AMERICAN HISTORY
FOR EVERYONE

AMERICAN HISTORY

FOR EVERYONE

The Fascinating Story
of Our Great Nation

RICHARD LEDERER

First Printing, 2024

ISBN-13: 978-1-962984-51-5 print edition
ISBN-13: 978-1-962984-52-2 e-book edition

Waterside Productions
2055 Oxford Ave
Cardiff, CA 92007
www.waterside.com

to my grandparents, Yankel and Rivka Perewosky
and William and Nettie Lederer,
for coming to America

to my grandchildren,
Maud, Mattias, Leo, Lucy, Nellie, Isaac, and Zoe

and to Bill and Gayle Gladstone, who made this book possible

Table of Contents

INTRODUCTION

This is America — a brilliant diversity spread like stars,
a thousand points of light in a broad and peaceful sky.
GEORGE H.W. BUSH, *41ˢᵗ president*

More than a decade ago, I birthed three small popular history books, *American Trivia, Presidential Trivia,* and *American Trivia Quiz Book.* That experience put me in touch with some of the most fascinating and compelling truths about America, its history, and its people. Above all, it reminded me that, while we Americans are of many backgrounds, we are one people, united through a common experience. I've always wanted to tell that story.

Newscasters and politicians like to exaggerate our differences and divisions in America. But if you take a closer look, you'll see there's a lot more that binds us together than separates us. Ultimately, history is about people — their experiences, their lives, and their stories.

Come join me on a bumpy ride through the fascinating historical highlights of our first four hundred years. I'm guessing that this trip will inspire you to reflect more deeply on the strands of human experience that have been woven together to create our country's grand tapestry and about what kind of social fabric you want to leave to those who come after you.

So what are the ties that unite a nation as vast, far-reaching, and diverse as ours? We are not a people made from a single stock. Rather, we are a medley of colors, races, religions, and ethnicities. As Jesse Jackson explains, "Our flag is red, white, and blue, but our nation is a rainbow — red, yellow, brown, black, and white." President Barack Obama adds, "Our patchwork heritage is a strength, not a weakness. We are a nation of Christians and Muslims, Jews and Hindus, and non-believers. We are shaped by every language and culture, drawn from every end of this earth."

You might think our English language unites us, but, in fact, we have no official language. We actually speak all the languages of the world. Walking down the street in any American city, you may hear Spanish (our second most spoken language) or Chinese or Yiddish or any of the more than eight hundred other tongues.

We share a nation with many people who may look different from us; speak languages different from ours; share rituals, customs, and foods different from ours; and worship in ways that may seem strange to us. What, then, holds us together in this vast and varied land of ours?

The one thing we Americans have in common is our history. It doesn't matter if you're a first-generation or twelfth-generation American. You own our history. That's what makes you an American. That's the glue that binds us together.

Most of us learn a smattering of that history in school. Then, like so much of what we acquired back then, the chronicle of our national adventure fades into the background of our lives. Historians Will and Ariel Durant point out: "We Americans are the best-informed people on earth as to the events of the last twenty-four hours. We are not the best informed as to the events of the past sixty centuries."

Recent surveys reveal that one quarter of Americans think that Christopher Columbus set sail after 1750, and one-third can't identify the century in which the Revolutionary War was fought. Three-quarters of respondents do not know that America achieved its independence from Great Britain.

Only 7 percent can name the first four presidents of the United States in order (Washington, Adams, Jefferson, and Madison), and only 21 percent know that the faces of Thomas Jefferson, George Washington, Abraham Lincoln, and Theodore Roosevelt are carved on Mount Rushmore. But more than half of Americans can name at least two members of the Simpsons' cartoon family.

I wrote this book to make the knowledge of our nation's history at least match the nation's knowledge of the Simpsons.

I hope *American History for Everyone* will make the history of America come to life for you — that you'll think more about the diverse people who have gone before us and worked so hard to bequeath us a united, spirited, and enchanting country blessed with the gifts of life, liberty, and the pursuit of happiness.

richardhlederer@gmail.com/verbivore.com

PART I
ORIGINS

America was not built on fear.
America was built on courage, on imagination,
and an unbeatable determination to do the job at hand.
HARRY S. TRUMAN, *33rd president*

CHAPTER 1
HOW WE GOT OUR NAME

Perhaps there is a continent or a very large country
populated by human beings and animals as yet unseen.
AMERIGO VESPUCCI, *Mundus Novus, 1504*

C hristopher Columbus (1451-1506) generally gets credit for finding America. In grade school, many of us learned this ditty:

In fourteen hundred ninety two,
Columbus sailed the ocean blue.

And he did.
On his first
voyage, he
sighted the
Bahamas
and made
land on His-
paniola
(now Haiti
and the
Dominican Re-
public). On three subsequent voyages (1493, 1498, 1502), he also
explored the coast of South America. But Columbus never realized
that he had sailed to the New World. He died in 1506, blissfully
certain that he had reached Asia. An Italian, Amerigo Vespucci
(1454-1512), working in Spain for the Medici family, helped outfit
the ships for Columbus's first voyage. He in turn made two voyages

to the New World, although never to North America, in 1499 and 1501. When he returned to Spain, he wrote about the wonders he had seen.

His account was widely read, even in the Duchy of Lorraine (now part of eastern France), where Dutch cartographer Martin Waldseemüller (1470?-1520) was drawing a new map of the world. Waldseemüller decided to write the name *America* across the face of the new continent on his map. He wished to honor Vespucci as the first to recognize that South America was a separate continent, not part of Asia. He wrote, "And Amerigo Vespucci has found another, fourth part [separate from Europe, Africa, and Asia], for which I see no reason why anyone could properly disapprove of a name derived from that of Amerigo, the discoverer, a man of sagacious genius." Waldseemüller published a thousand copies of his map in 1507. As far as we know, only one survives, now housed in the Library of Congress.

By the way, *Amerigo* is the Italian form of the Medieval Latin name *Emericus*, which was, in turn, derived from the German *Heimirich* — *Henry* in English.

See Waldseemüller's map at:

https://www.loc.gov/collections/discovery-and-exploration/articles-and-essays/recognizing-and-naming-america/

CHAPTER 2
OUR EARLIEST IMMIGRANTS

> We were the original "Americans," indigenous people
> who have inhabited these shores for over 20,000 years.
> JACQUELINE KEELER, *Navajo/Yankton Dakota Sioux writer*

When Columbus "discovered" the New World, he actually came late to the party.

There are dozens of theories posited about pre-Columbian transoceanic exploration of the Americas from Europe, Asia, Africa, and Oceania, but most are speculative. There are no supporting data.

There is, however, firm evidence of Vikings building short-lived settlement we call L'Anse aux Meadows in Newfoundland. Some of the items found there are tree-ring dated to the year 1021 C.E. But even they were late. A group of immigrants arrived possibly thirty thousand years before them, and they stayed. We call their descendants "Indians" or "Native Americans."

Each Native American tribe or group has its own origin story. Many of those origin stories involve the people being created where they now live. Science suggests an alternate version.

Scientists agree that humans most likely came into North America from Siberia. They weren't paid explorers seeking wealth for their employers or seeking to spread the Christian gospel; they were hunter-gatherers following their food sources, migrating herds of grazers.

What scientists haven't figured out yet is when they came. For many years, the accepted date was about thirteen thousand years ago, but new tools, techniques, and archaeological sites with persuasive evidence have changed everything. So not

5

thirteen thousand, but maybe as many as thirty-five thousand years ago. As more information becomes available, scientists will work toward an agreement on dates.

One thing we can say for sure, though, is that when Columbus arrived in 1492, indigenous people had spread across North, Central, and South America and to the islands offshore.

Estimates are that in North America in 1492, around six hundred tribes that spoke between three hundred and five hundred languages existed, which is to say that there were between three hundred and five hundred distinct cultures with diverse ideas, goals, and lifeways. Unlike what current popular culture implies, not all Native Americans wore feathers, rode horses, or chased buffalo.

There are currently 574 federally recognized tribes in the lower forty-eight states and Alaska, and they are as varied as their ancestors were.

Back in 1492, when Columbus first touched the shore of San Salvador in the Bahamas, the population of Europe — the Old World — was about sixty million. Population estimates for the New World are more difficult. Estimates are based on archaeological and other scientific data. They range between 43 million and 112 million indigenous people in the Americas.

Scholars estimate that there were between 3.8 million and 10 million people in what is now the United States and Canada. Although absolute numbers are questionable, what we know is that in the one hundred years after first contact with Europeans, the indigenous population crashed. Many areas were totally depopulated. As many as 90 percent died from European diseases, such as smallpox, measles, the common cold, influenza, and syphilis, in addition to violence; starvation; and slavery.

An early example of the devastation of disease is the story of Tisquantum, more commonly known as Squanto. He was a member of the Wampanoag Patuxent tribe. He learned English and acted as a translator and liaison between his tribe of approximately two thousand people and the Mayflower Pilgrims. Captured by a slaver in 1614, he was taken to Spain and sold. There, monks took him to be educated and Christianized. He returned to North America in 1619 to find that all the members of his tribe were gone, dead from disease.

Native Americans enslaved other Native Americans before contact with Europeans, but with cross-Atlantic contact came the profit motive. The Europeans needed a labor force larger than they could supply themselves. Also, they wanted to exploit the land of the indigenous people to make way for their own use. Slavery of both Native Americans and, later, Africans were their answer to the problems. Both Europeans and Native Americans took and sold enslaved people. Enslaved Native Americans who stayed in the colonies often escaped captivity. Some ran back to their tribes, others to Canada, where their descendants still live. A large number were taken to islands in the Caribbean, from which it was harder to escape, and their descendants make up part of the present-day population there.

As with other population figures, accurate tallies for the total number of Native Americans enslaved in the North American colonies and states in the seventeenth through the nineteenth century are difficult to pin down, but there may have been as high as 5.5 million.

Chapter 3
Of Human Bondage

> Notwithstanding my grandmother's
> long and faithful service to her owners,
> not one of her children escaped the auction block.
> These God-breathing machines are no more,
> in the sight of their masters,
> than the cotton they plant, or the horses they tend.
> HARRIET ANN JACOBS, *Incidents in the Life of a Slave Girl*

The first enslaved people imported into a British colony in what would become the United States were offloaded from a British-owned ship at Point Comfort, a few miles from the colony of Jamestown, Virginia, in August 1619.

They weren't the first slaves in the Americas. Many of the early Spanish explorers had slaves with them. Some Native Americans tribes enslaved other slaved other Native Americans — generally war captives, sometimes debtors — and British colonists also enslaved indigenous people. Ultimately, Spanish, French, Dutch, and English colonists in all the islands of the Caribbean, New Spain, Brazil, Canada, and all thirteen American colonies practiced slavery.

Those first twenty people who were offloaded had been kidnapped and enslaved in the African country of Angola. They may have been slaves, but not necessarily under the conditions that became common later. Some of them may have even been considered a type of indentured servant. Indentured servants signed contracts to work for masters for a term of time to pay off the cost of bringing them to the Americas and for the cost of their keep during their indenture — usually no more than seven years. After that, they were free. Masters were required to either pay them or give them land to farm.

Most indentured servants came from England. Gradually the system shifted away from indenture toward slavery because indentured servants had such a high mortality rate that they had to be replaced often. That was expensive. Also, as word came back to England about how difficult life was in the colonies, fewer people were willing to sign up for indenture.

There was also a shift from indigenous Native American slaves to African slaves. It was easier for indigenous slaves to escape — they were on "home territory" — and they were more susceptible to deadly European diseases than the Africans were.

Slaves, at that time, were effectively indentured for life, but their children were free. However, the story of slavery in what became the United States is actually multiple stories, not just one. Each colony and territory had its own local government, rules, laws, and customs, and those all changed over time.

In its final form in the United States, slaves were still enslaved for life, but under law, their children now took on the status of the mother. Children of a slave mother were also enslaved for life, without regard to who their father was. Few white fathers acknowledged their slave children or emancipated them. This shift to the child taking the status of the mother was a major change in law. Previously, under law, men were responsible for their children, but no longer.

In the end, it was cheaper for a slave owner to breed his own slaves, as he or she would breed cattle or horses, than it was to buy new ones, so enslaved women were forced to produce babies. Sometimes they had a say about who the father(s) of their children would be, sometimes not. Some slave women resisted by causing self-abortions or committing infanticide so that their children would not be doomed to a life of slavery.

Slaveholders exerted absolute control over their slaves. Slaves were considered chattels — personal property. The owners could sell them or their children, abuse, punish, or even kill them at will. Slaves had no recourse through the law.

Enslaved people resisted. Some slaves maimed themselves so that they couldn't work. Some ran away in groups or individually; that created a new job description: slave catcher. Suicide rates among slaves were high. And history records more than 250 slave rebellions (defined as more than ten slaves participating) in North America during the seventeenth, eighteenth, and nineteenth centuries. Most of those rebellions involved the deaths of some slaveholders and the torture and execution of accused slave conspirators. Slaveholders lived in constant fear of those rebellions.

In most of the northern colonies, slaves generally worked as house servants, artisans, laborers, and craftsmen. In New York and the southern colonies, they primarily worked as field hands. Cash crops — indigo, tobacco, and rice in the South (and much later, cotton) and wheat, corn, flax, and tobacco in New York — were labor intensive. Workers were in great demand.

Initially, slaves were expensive. Only wealthy people could afford them, but as the supply of African slaves increased, prices came down, and people with less wealth were able to buy them.

Great Britain, Denmark-Norway, the Dutch Republic, France, Portugal, Spain, and Sweden began to participate in the Atlantic slave trade. In the late seventeenth century and eighteenth century, the British East India Company even brought several thousand East Indian slaves to some of the southern colonies, primarily Virginia and South Carolina, but African slaves were cheaper, so they gave up the practice.

Ultimately, approximately 388,000 Africans were enslaved, transported, and sold in the American colonies, a small percentage of the twelve and a half million Africans who were transported and sold in the Americas as a whole. Transporting slaves into the U.S. became illegal in 1808.

CHAPTER 4
WE THE PEOPLE GATHER

My fellow Americans,
we are and always will be a nation of immigrants.
We were strangers once, too.
BARACK OBAMA, *44th president*

Each of our thirteen colonies had its own reason for being. Some groups colonized places where they hoped to find freedom for themselves, not necessarily for everyone. Others aimed to make profits for absentee owners. One colony, Georgia, was a place for working off prison sentences. All colonists sought to better their lot in life.

New England Colonies
★ Colony of Rhode Island and Providence Plantations
★ Province of New Hampshire
★ Connecticut Colony
★ Province of Massachusetts Bay

Middle Colonies:
★ Province of New York
★ Province of Pennsylvania
★ Province of New Jersey
★ Delaware Colony

Southern Colonies:
★ Province of Maryland
★ Province of North Carolina

★ Colony of Virginia

★ Province of South Carolina

★ Province of Georgia

In 1682, William Penn established Philadelphia on the principles of freedom and religious tolerance. Ninety-four years later, in 1776, it was a city of between thirty and forty thousand people.

It was the largest city in the Americas north of Mexico City. New York, at the time, had approximately five thousand residents. Boston had approximately seven thousand. Philadelphia was the second largest English-speaking city in the world, after London; and the third most important commercial center in the British Empire, after London and Liverpool.

The thirty-to-forty thousand people in Philadelphia were remarkably diverse. They included Whites, Blacks, and a small number of Native Americans, mostly of the Lenape tribe.

We don't have exact data, because the first official census of the Unites States didn't happen until fourteen years later, in 1790. However, historical research into general trends of the time indicates that slightly more than fifty percent of those people were children under the age of sixteen. At the same time, the population included slightly more females than males. Except for the Lenape, whose ancestors had been there for thousands of years, some of those residents were the fourth or fifth generation of families that had settled in Philadelphia in William Penn's time. They or their ancestors came from many different places:

Each colony had its distinctive character and population, but focusing on Philadelphia will give us a sense of what a nation of varied people the United States was from its very beginning.

★ England (approximately 30%)

★ Finland

★ Scotland/Ireland (20%)

★ the Kingdom of France

★ Holy Roman Empire (now Germany - 15%)

★ Sweden

★ West Africa: enslaved and freedmen

★ Swiss Confederacy

★ the Dutch Republic (now the Netherlands)

★ Wales

Because Philadelphia was a major port city, people from many other countries and ethnicities often mixed with the residents. Ships came to Philadelphia from the American Eastern Seaboard, the Caribbean, Europe, and Africa.

Besides being diverse, in both ethnicity and nationality, the populace was religiously tolerant. Protestant Christians, (Anglicans, Quakers, Presbyterians, Lutherans and Pietists, Baptists, Dutch and German Reformed, Amish, Moravians, Mennonites, and Huguenots) made up about 60% of the people. The rest were Roman Catholic, Jewish, (non-Christian) Deists, or unaffiliated. The Lenape population maintained their traditional animist beliefs, sometimes blended with Christianity. Some of the African Americans were Christian while others were Muslim. A third contingent maintained their traditional African religions or mingled them with Christianity.

Job opportunities for colonial men included farmer; buyer, seller, and trader of goods that came into or went out of the port; ship builder; sail-maker; roper; sailor, dockhand; blacksmith;

carpenter; cooper, mason, carter, cook, printer (Benjamin Franklin got his start here); leatherworker; tailor; porter; and servant. Men ran taverns, breweries, bakeries, and stables. Educated men had opportunities in law, the ministry, medicine, finance, and politics.

Colonial women weren't sitting on their hands either. Some wives worked in their husbands' businesses. But more than that, the 1790 census showed that women headed one in every eight households in Philadelphia. A few were independently wealthy, having inherited from their fathers or husbands, but most of these women had to work to feed their families. They ran boarding or lodging houses, coffee houses, taverns, stores, or stands at markets. They worked as servants, cooks, laundresses, nurses, midwives, schoolmistresses, spinners, tailors, chandlers, weavers, mantua (dress) makers, madams, and prostitutes.

CHAPTER 5
OUR NATION'S BIRTH CERTIFICATE

The decree is gone forth, and it cannot be recalled,
that a more equal liberty
than has prevailed in other parts of the earth
must be established in America.
JOHN ADAMS, *2nd president*

The Fourth of July is the most prominent all-American holiday — the birthday of our country — even though celebrating the Fourth didn't become common until after 1815, and Independence Day wasn't made a federal holiday until 1870.

Do we ever celebrate! Families gather for parades, picnics, concerts, carnivals, and fireworks.

That national outpouring of jubilation commemorates the signing of the Declaration of Independence. But if you have an image in your mind of a room full of patriots lined up to sign that document on the fourth, think again. That's not how it happened.

When Payton Randolph (1721-1775) of Virginia gaveled the Second Continental Congress to order on May 10, 1775, it was only three weeks after the battles against the British at Lexington and Concord, Massachusetts (April 19). Representatives from all thirteen colonies attended this meeting of the de facto national government. Even so, the delegates had little appetite for breaking away from England. Instead, in July 1775, they sent a petition to King George III asking him to protect them from Parliament, which, in the colonists' eyes, taxed them often and unreasonably. No colonist sat in Parliament. The phrase "no taxation without representation" summed up their complaint. King George ignored their petition.

16

On June 11, 1776, the Congress named Benjamin Franklin of Pennsylvania, John Adams of Massachusetts, Roger Sherman of Connecticut, Robert Livingston of New York, and Thomas Jefferson of Virginia to form a committee to draft an affirmation of independence. Jefferson took on the role of writing the first draft of the declaration.

It was in the Declaration of Independence that the term *The United States of America* first appeared. All Americans probably know the clarion words of the preamble: "We hold these truths to be self-evident, that all men are created equal, that they are endowed by their Creator with certain unalienable Rights, that among these are Life, Liberty, and the pursuit of Happiness."

That statement has been called "one of the best-known sentences in the English language" and "the most potent and consequential words in American history."

After some revisions, the Continental Congress on July 2 voted to accept the declaration of our national sovereignty. As reported in the Pennsylvania *Evening Post,* "This day the Continental Congress declared the United Colonies Free and Independent States."

On the fourth, John Hancock (1737-1793) of Massachusetts, president of the Congress, signed the Declaration of Independence with his prodigious signature in an almost empty chamber. Secretary Charles Thomson was the only other person who actually signed the declaration on July 4, as a witness to Hancock's signature.

On July 8, Hancock read the text to a large and boisterous crowd in Philadelphia. Their joyful response was the first celebration of American independence. On July 19, Congress ordered that the Declaration of Independence be engrossed on parchment. That completed, the engrosser returned it to John Hancock to be signed. Forty-nine delegates signed it on August

2, almost a month after its adoption. Five signed it later, and two never signed.

That document marked the formal end of the effort by the American colonies to reconcile with King George. We now considered ourselves an independent nation, no longer subjects of the British king and no longer the United Colonies.

The original parchment copy of the Declaration of Independence reposes, with the Constitution and the Bill of Rights, in the National Archives in Washington, D.C.

You can see them at:

https://www.archives.gov/founding-docs/declaration

CHAPTER 6

HOME OF THE BRAVE

The tree of liberty must be refreshed
From time to time with the blood of patriots.
THOMAS JEFFERSON, *3rd president*

When we learned American history in school, it was in a series of snapshots like the old family pictures in our parents' photo albums — strangers in odd-looking clothes and hairstyles, looking stiff and uncomfortable. Those pictures gave no clue as to the ideas and passions that guided those lives. And make no mistake; they were as passionate about life as we are.

Life often calls on us to be heroes, sometimes in small ways, sometimes in grand ways. A hero is a person admired for courage, nobility, exploits, qualities, or achievements and regarded as an ideal or model. America seems to be good at making heroes when we need them. We see them in our daily lives: the police officer, the firefighter, the soldier, and the crusader for a just cause. Sometimes they rise to astonishing heights when circumstances require it.

Here are some heroes of our Revolutionary War (1775-1783) you may not have heard about, and like America itself, they are of many heritages, backgrounds, and beliefs. No matter whether they were male or female; Black, Brown, or White; animist, atheist, Christian, Deist, Jew, Muslim, or other non-Christian; recent immigrant or with deeper roots — they all contributed to this great experiment we call American Democracy.

★ Crispus Attucks (c. 1723-1770) died in the Boston Massacre and is considered by many to be the first casualty of the Revolutionary War and our first Black American hero. He may have been either a freedman or an escaped slave at the time of his death. He was of mixed African and Wampanoag Indian descent and was described as a "mulatto" in contemporary publications. He earned his living as a sailor and whaler.

In 1767, the British Parliament imposed a set of taxes, the Townshend Duties, on the American colonies — another in a series of taxes the Americans considered "taxation without representation." Tensions were high in Boston. Britain stationed troops there in 1768 to try to dampen the growing political unrest. That only increased it.

The fracas that became the massacre on March 5, 1770, began with a thirteen-year-old wigmaker's apprentice harassing a British officer over what he thought was an unpaid bill. A British sentry came to the officer's aid. A crowd of three to four hundred Bostonians gathered. Eight other British troops arrived to protect the sentry and started firing into the crowd. Five men, including Attucks, died. Six more were wounded.

★ Margaret Cochran Corbin (1751-1800), the daughter of an Irish immigrant, became a hero at the Battle of Fort Washington in northern Manhattan on November 16, 1776. As many wives did, she followed her husband, John, while he served in the army. She cooked and washed for him and helped tend the wounded. Additionally, she carried water to soldiers in battle. She may have been the first person to carry the nickname "Molly Pitcher."

The battle shaped up with 2,800 Americans facing 8,000 Hessians (mercenary soldiers from six German territories in the Holy Roman Empire). John Corbin and another soldier manned one of two cannons at the fort. When they were killed, Margaret took their place. Although she was not trained to the work, she had seen it so often that she was able to do it well. Seriously wounded at her post, she was taken prisoner by the British when the fort fell. She was paroled because of her wounds. Margaret was permanently disabled and became the first woman in America to receive a military pension.

★ Another woman with a similar battle history was Mary Ludwig Hayes (1754-1832), who became a hero during the Battle of Monmouth (New Jersey) on June 28, 1778. She also carried water to soldiers on the battlefield. In that battle and others, it was as common for soldiers to die of heat and dehydration as to die from their wounds. Hayes is another candidate for the original holder of the nickname "Molly Pitcher."

★ Nathan Hale (1755-1776) of Connecticut, a Yale-educated teacher, became a captain in the Continental Army and a member of a select group of fighters called Knowlton's Rangers, the first organized intelligence service. He volunteered to go through the British lines to gather intelligence on troop positions in New York City. He was smuggled into the city on September 15, 1776. There, a Loyalist recognized and reported him. He was captured on the twenty-first and hanged as a spy the next day without benefit of clergy or a Bible, although he requested both. At twenty-one years of age, he went bravely to his death, saying, "I only regret that I have but one life to lose for my country."

★ James Armistead Lafayette (1748–1830) was born enslaved in Virginia. His master allowed him to join the Continental Army. There, he worked for French General Marquis de Lafayette. (After the war, James added Lafayette to his name to honor the general.)

In 1781, posing as a runaway slave, he was sent to attach himself to the Virginia camp of Benedict Arnold, after Arnold turned traitor to the American cause. He earned Arnold's trust. Later, he moved on to the camp of British General Lord Charles Cornwallis. Acting as a double agent in both places, he fed misinformation to the British and true information to the Americans. The intelligence he supplied was vital to the American victory at Yorktown, the final and possibly most important battle of the war.

Virginia's slaves had been promised freedom by the Virginia legislature if they served, but after the war, that was modified. Only those who carried a gun were freed. James did not qualify. He petitioned the legislature twice, and finally, with Lafayette's personal recommendation, won his freedom.

★ Sybil Ludington (1761-1839), like Paul Revere, rode horseback in the dark of night. On April 26, 1777, at the age of sixteen, she rode forty miles through a rainstorm to find her father, Henry, a colonel in the New York militia, and warn him that the British planned an attack on Danbury, Connecticut. Unlike Revere two years earlier, she was not captured and completed her mission. Although the British were successful in their attack, her warning gave the Americans time to regroup and finally drive the Redcoats back to the Long Island Sound. The Post Office included her in a series of stamps published to celebrate the bicentennial in 1975. The series, called "Contributors to the Cause," also included Haym Soloman and Salem Poor.

★ Salem Poor (1747–1802) was born enslaved to the Poor family in the Province of Massachusetts Bay. Although records were not kept on the religious affiliations of enslaved people, it's considered likely that he was Muslim. Some scholars estimate that as many as one third of slaves brought from western and central Africa were Muslim. Although many were forced to convert to Christianity, some were allowed to keep their religion.

Slaves were sometimes allowed to take side jobs to earn cash. Poor did and bought his freedom in 1769, paying the equivalent of a year's earnings of an average working man. It was a major accomplishment that he was able to save that much money by the age of twenty-two.

Poor joined the militia in 1775 as one of the famed minutemen and later joined the Continental Army. He saw action in the Battle of Bunker Hill (actually Breed's Hill) near Boston along with at least three dozen other African American soldiers. Fourteen officers commended him in writing for valor and gallantry. He also participated at Valley Forge and in the Battles of White Plains, Saratoga, and Monmouth.

The Revolutionary War was the only time the American Army was fully integrated until 165 years later, when, in 1948, President Harry S. Truman signed an executive order stating, "There shall be equality of treatment and opportunity for all persons in the armed forces without regard to race, color, religion, or national origin."

★ Haym Salomon (1740-1785) was a Polish-born Jew who lived and worked in New York City. The British arrested him as a spy in 1776. Pardoned, he was hired to work as an interpreter for the British with their Hessian mercenary troops. Salomon secretly encouraged soldiers to desert, acted as a spy, and helped prisoners escape. Arrested again in 1778, tried, and sentenced to death, he escaped to Philadelphia, where he helped finance the Revolution, by lending large sums of his own money to the fledgling country and arranging loans from France.

Salomon was paymaster for the six-thousand-man French army under the command of Count de Rochambeau that fought beside the Continental Army, and he personally resupplied and rearmed the American troops at Yorktown, the decisive battle of the War.

Salomon died at age forty-four, deeply in debt. The financially strapped American government had been unable to repay the money he had provided.

★ Deborah Sampson (1762-1827) disguised herself as Robert Shurtliff (her dead brother) and joined the Fourth Massachusetts Regiment. The army stationed her in New York and assigned her to the Light Infantry, a lightly equipped mobile company that functioned as scouts, raiders, and skirmishers to harass the enemy. Wounded in battle, she avoided medical care rather than risk discovery and extracted one pistol ball by herself. She couldn't reach a second bullet. It remained, and the wound never healed properly.

She served for nearly two years without being found out. This isn't as strange as it sounds. Soldiers slept in their clothes and rarely bathed. In October 1783, she grew ill during an epidemic and was taken to a hospital where her true gender was recognized. She received an honorable discharge, petitioned for a pension, and ultimately received it. After her death, her husband successfully petitioned for a pension as the spouse of a deceased soldier.

★ A number of other women also served disguised as men, including women like Anna Maria Lane (1755-1810). Disguised as a man, she joined the army with her husband, John, in 1776 and served until 1781. She fought in a number of battles and was wounded at the Battle of Germantown (Pennsylvania). Like other women, she didn't get treatment for fear of discovery. The wound plagued her the rest of her life.

In their old age, the couple petitioned the Virginia legislature for pensions. John received $40 per year. Anna Maria received $100 per year, perhaps a sign that she had done something unusually heroic. Records don't tell us what.

★ Friedrich Wilhelm von Steuben (1730-1794) was a Prussian military officer recruited by Benjamin Franklin and hired by George Washington in 1778 to reorganize and train the Continental Army into an effective fighting force. He received the rank of Major General. Historians believe Steuben was openly homosexual at a time when being gay was a crime meriting death. Washington chose to overlook it because of Steuben's desperately needed skills, and he became Washington's chief of staff and trusted advisor. He was successful in his mission and is now considered one of the founding fathers of the U.S. Army.

Historians estimate that there were a quarter of a million Native Americans in about eighty nations living east of the Mississippi River. These people were concerned with maintaining control of their own lands at a time when white settlers threatened to overwhelm them. Most of the native nations thought their best strategy during the war was to stay neutral. Others chose sides.

★ Tyonajanegan (c.173?-1822), also known as Two Kettles Together, was an Oneida Indian. Most of their tribe chose to support the American side. They first fought in the Battle of Oriskiny (New York) on August 6, 1777. The battle was between about eight hundred Patriots and more than fifty Oneidas against about five hundred Loyalists (to the British), Hessian mercenaries, Iroquois, and Mississaugas Indians. The Loyalists ambushed the Patriots and beat them badly. After the battle, the Iroquois attacked the Oneida village of Oriska and burned it, along with Tyonajanegan's farm, to the ground.

CHAPTER 7

THE SUPREME LAW OF OUR LAND

America is the only country in the world
founded on an idea,
an idea that all people are created equal
and deserve to be treated equally throughout their lives.
We've never lived up to that,
but we've never, ever, ever walked away from it.
JOSEPH BIDEN, *46ᵗʰ president*

Imagine the Constitutional Convention. The doors and windows of Independence Hall in Philadelphia are closed, protecting the men from the curiosity of those passing by outside. Not a breath of air stirs through the room. Flies buzz in lazy circles. The temperature is eighty-seven and the humidity is high. Sweat beads on faces.

All around, pairs of men sit at small tables. Some write. The soft scratches of their quill pens disturb neither the concentration of those who sit and think nor those who chat with their neighbors. All stop what they're doing and turn toward the front of the room as the president of the convention stands. George Washington (1732-1799) begins to speak. "Gentlemen, let us continue with our discussion. Dr. Franklin, I believe you have the floor."

If only we could have been there to experience that important milestone in the creation of our nation. The Constitutional Convention began on May 25, 1787. It seems so static when we read about it. In fact, it was alive with passionate debate as the delegates hammered out the details of our future. By mid-June 1787, it became clear that, rather than amending the existing Articles of Confederation, forged in 1781 to influence appears to be exerted by the Iroquois confederation. Their Great Law of Peace united six nations under a federal structure while each maintained internal autonomy. Additionally, the Iroquois laws included the separation of civil and military authority, checks and balances between different branches of government, a bicameral legislature with upper and lower houses, and a process for removing leaders from office. All of these elements found their way into the U.S. Constitution in some form.

The Constitution of the United States is the oldest written constitution in use in the world. Although we have amended the document twenty-seven times, we the people of the United States have never found it necessary to call for a second Constitutional Convention in all the years since.

Over time, the engrossed parchment on which the Constitution is inscribed has lived in several different places. In 1952, an armored tank under military guard carried our Constitution from the Library of Congress to the National Archives, where it remains in a shrine in the rotunda, alongside the Bill of Rights and the Declaration of Independence

CHAPTER 8

THE FATHER OF OUR COUNTRY

I walk on untrodden ground.
There is scarcely any part of my conduct
which may not hereafter be drawn into precedent.
GEORGE WASHINGTON, *1ˢᵗ president*

George Washington was born in Virginia on February 11, 1731, according to the Julian calendar,

The British and the French were competing for control of the Ohio River Valley. Washington's first assignment was to liaise with the Iroquois Confederacy to gather intelligence about the French and to deliver a message to the French near what later became Fort Duquesne (and even later Pittsburgh). The message was that they should leave the valley. He delivered his message to the French commander, who refused the ultimatum. Washington returned to Virginia, completing the mission in seventy-seven days in difficult winter conditions. His report was published in Virginia and London and brought him public attention.

His marriage to wealthy widow Martha Dandridge Custis in 1759 made him one of the richest and most famous people in Virginia. As he became more convinced of the rightness of the patriot cause, he used that popularity to become more active in politics. He was ultimately sent as a representative from Virginia to both the First and Second Continental Congresses.

The Revolutionary War started on April 19, 1775. Washington was appointed by the Congress as "General & Commander in chief of the army of the United Colonies and of all the forces raised or to be raised by them." His skills as a commander led to the Patriots ousting the British. Peace finally came exactly eight years later on April 19, 1783.

On December 23, 1783, General George Washington resigned his commission as commander-in-chief of the Continental army.

★   After unanimously electing Washington president in 1789, members of Congress faced a new challenge: deciding how to address him. Having never elected a president, other countries offered no precedent. Suggestions included "His Exalted Highness," "His Elected Highness," "His Majesty the President," and "His Highness, the President of the United States, and Protector of the Rights of the Same." Washington would have none of that, and he decided that he would simply be called "Mr. President."

★ Washington did not sign the Declaration of Independence because, as Commander-in-Chief of the Continental Army, he was busy defending New York City from the British. John Adams and Thomas Jefferson were the only future presidents to sign it. Thirteen years later, George Washington and James Madison were the only future presidents to sign the Constitution.

★ From Washington to Dwight Eisenhower, thirteen presidents were generals. In 1976, President Gerald Ford, as part of America's bicentennial celebration, posthumously promoted George Washington to "General of the Armies of the United States," a rank forever above all other officers of the U.S. Army. U.S. Representative Lucien Nedzl thought the rank was unnecessary, saying, "It's like the Pope offering to make Christ a Cardinal."

★ Washington (both terms) and James Monroe (second term) were the only two presidents to run unopposed. They are also our only two presidents who have national capitals named after them — Washington, D.C., and Monrovia, Liberia. George Washington is the only president after whom a state is named, while four state capitals commemorate other presidents — Jefferson City, Missouri; Madison, Wisconsin; Jackson, Mississippi; and Lincoln, Nebraska.

★ George Washington suffered severe tooth loss that made it difficult for him to eat and even speak. At his inauguration, Washington had but a single tooth that was his. At various times he wore dentures made of human teeth, animal teeth, or lead. It's sometimes claimed that he had wooden teeth, but that's not true. Wood would have rotted. His lack of choppers altered the shape of his once-handsome face, resulting in the pinched look in his later portraits.

★ In 1796, George Washington retired after four decades of public service, including two terms as our first president. He declined to serve a third term. Washington returned to Mount Vernon, Virginia, to devote his attention to making his plantation as productive as it had been before he became president. He died on December 14, 1799, at the age of sixty-seven. He was entombed at Mount Vernon. His eulogy was written and delivered by his good friend Major-General Henry "Light Horse Harry" Lee. He famously said of Washington, "First in war, first in peace, and first in the hearts of his countrymen."

PART II
MONUMENTS AND SYMBOLS

It was the rampant, patriotic display which struck me,
waving flags and blaring oratory.
My country was the real thing,
the monument was indeed a lofty reality.
SYLVIA PLATH, *poet and novelist,*
on seeing the Lincoln Memorial

CHAPTER 9
FLYING COLORS

The red and white and starry blue
Is freedom's shield and hope
JOHN PHILIP SOUSA, composer and conductor

Monuments and symbols are shorthand for complex and passionate ideas and experiences. They possess an importance beyond their physical existence. Sometimes they're created deliberately, as were the American flag and the Washington Monument. Other times they grow from their context and proximity to history, like the Liberty Bell.

Our red, white, and blue American flag is the most visible symbol of our nation. Walk through any downtown, and you will see the flag flying at the post office, the police station, the fire station, and any number of commercial buildings. Walk through any neighborhood, and you may see a flag flying in front of a home. People wear flag pins and flag-themed clothes. Cars sport flag decals. And the flag's stars, stripes, and colors appear on many products in our stores, including the covers of this book.

The Second Continental Congress officially adopted our flag on

June 14, 1777. The law read, "that the flag of the thirteen United States be thirteen stripes alternate red and white: that the union be thirteen stars, white in a blue field, representing a new constellation." The flag served as a maritime flag, used exclusively to identify

American ships, until 1834, when the army adopted it as a battle flag. It didn't become a symbol of the nation as a whole until much later.

The thirteen stars and stripes of the original flag symbolized the number of original states, but the flag has been modified twenty-six times since 1777. President William Howard Taft mandated the first formal specifications, other than that the stars had to be five-pointed, in 1912. President Dwight Eisenhower established the current flag specifications by executive order on August 21, 1959, the day Hawaii joined the union as our fiftieth state. In 1960, the current fifty-star version was adopted.

The creation of the American flag is one of the classic stories of the founding of the United States. Some historians give credit to Francis Hopkinson, one of the signers of the Declaration of Independence as a delegate from New Jersey; but the story of Betsy Ross (1752-1836) seems to have captured the imaginations of more Americans. And although there is scant historical proof of the specifics of the story, there is agreement about the course of Betsy's life.

She was born Elizabeth Griscom, the eighth of seventeen children, on January 1, 1752. She was a fourth-generation American, raised as a Quaker and apprenticed to an upholsterer. At twenty-one, she eloped with John Ross, a fellow apprentice. Betsy and John opened an upholstery shop in Philadelphia, where they did general sewing for the home.

These were times of political ferment. When the Revolutionary War flared up in 1775, John Ross joined a militia. He died in January 1776, when a cache of gunpowder he was guarding on the waterfront exploded. After two years of marriage, Betsy was a childless war widow struggling to keep her upholstery business alive.

As the story goes, in May a committee of the Continental Congress composed of George Washington, Robert Morris, and George Ross, her late husband's uncle, came to Betsy and asked her to make a flag following a sketch that Washington had created. Betsy suggested alterations to the design, in particular changing the six-pointed stars to five-pointed since she could create them with one snip of her scissors. The committee was impressed with Betsy's demonstration, and she began her task and created the first American flag in June 1776. She continued to make American flags for another fifty years as part of her business.

Married and widowed twice more, Betsy Ross bore seven daughters. She retired in 1827, turning the business over to family and nine years later died at the age of eighty-four.

Visit the Betsy Ross House at:
https://historicphiladelphia.org/stories/did-she-or-didnt-she/

and learn to cut the Betsy Ross star at:
https://www.ushistory.org/betsy/flagstar.html

CHAPTER 10
A CAPITAL IDEA

Washington is a city of monuments, museums, and minds.
JAMES C. McCLENDON, *National Endowment for the Humanities*

B etween 1776 and 1800, our young government moved the capital thirteen times to nine different locations, sometimes just ahead of British troops — this was wartime. Those locations included Baltimore, Philadelphia, Lancaster, York, Princeton, Annapolis, Trenton, New York City, and, finally, Washington, D.C.

In 1788 and 1789, Maryland and Virginia together donated a hundred square miles of land for a capital city. While in office, our first president signed a bill establishing a future, permanent U.S. capital along the Potomac River. Construction was completed in 1800.

Ironically, the only president who didn't live in Washington was George Washington. During his administration (1789-1797), the nation's capital was first in New York and then Philadelphia. New York City was the capital on March 4, 1789, when we first started operating under the Constitution, and on April 30, when Washington was inaugurated the first time.

John Adams (1797-1801) was the first to occupy the President's House at 1600 Pennsylvania Avenue. The Adams family moved into their new home on November 1, 1800, while the paint was still drying. The family occupied it for only four months, having lived most of Adams' term in Philadelphia.

Capital Facts

★ The White House, previously called the President's

 House or the Executive Mansion, received its current name from Theodore Roosevelt in 1901, when he directed that all letterheads and documents use that term. It is the most-visited building in the United States. Graceland, Elvis Presley's former home, is second.

★ The Smithsonian Institution in Washington, D.C., the largest museum complex in the world, includes museums, galleries, research centers, and 160 affiliate museums around the world. Established in 1846 and enabled by the bequest of English chemist James Smithson, the Smithsonian comprises sixteen museums in Washington. With all these museums, it's no wonder that the Smithsonian is sometimes called "the Nation's Attic."

★ The Washington Monument honors George Washington and, in many people's eyes, symbolizes the city of Washington, D.C. Surrounded by fifty American flags, the monument stands near the west end of the National Mall. Towering approximately 555 feet, this marble obelisk is the tallest stone structure in the world.

The building of the monument began on July 4, 1848. Because of a lack of funds and, later, the Civil War, construction halted in 1856 and didn't resume for twenty years. The American centennial in 1876 inspired a national passion to complete the obelisk, a goal reached on December 6, 1884, when the final capstone was set.

Because marble quarried in one place was used between 1848 and 1856 and from another between 1876 and 1884, the marble of the bottom one-third is slightly different in color from the rest. The tip is constructed out of a material that, at the time, was unusual and expensive because it is so difficult to refine — aluminum!

★ The Library of Congress (where copies of this book will repose) is located in Washington, DC. The Congress used public libraries in New York and Philadelphia when the capital was located in those cities, but when they moved to Washington D.C., they realized that they'd have to create a library for their own use. Congress appropriated $5,000 to order 740 books and three maps from London.

The library had grown to three thousand volumes by the time the War of 1812 against the British and their Native American allies began. When the British took Washington D.C. in 1814, they burned many public buildings as payback for damage the American forces, including our Native American allies, had inflicted on Canada. At the end of the war, Thomas Jefferson sold his fifty-year collection of 6,487 books to the government for $23,950.

The library burned again in 1851. Around 35,000 books, two-thirds of the collection, were lost. The Congress finally authorized the construction of a separate fire-resistant building, the Thomas Jefferson Building, to house the collection.

Today, the Library of Congress houses about 173 million items and has over three thousand employees. This public research library is one of the largest in the world.

CHAPTER 11
NATIONAL SYMBOLS

Symbols speak a universal language
that can unite even the most diverse of nations
under a common source of pride.
MAYA ANGELOU, *poet and novelist*

National symbols can be things or ideas that are a shared language among the people of a country. They don't necessarily evoke the same emotion in each person, but each person understands what those symbols represent. Some are consciously designed or chosen to be symbols, for example, the Great Seal of the United States or the bald eagle. Others become symbolic because of their involvement in important historical events, such as the Alamo or Arlington National Cemetery. Still others are created as monuments to important events, such as the Iwo Jima Memorial, the World War II Memorial, the Korean War Veterans Memorial, or the Vietnam Veterans Memorial. These structures act to remind Americans of our history and point us to the future. Here are some of our more familiar symbols:

★ The Liberty Bell: In 1752, the colonial province of

Pennsylvania paid about $300 for a bell manufactured of copper, tin, lead, zinc, arsenic, gold, and silver and weighing 2,080 pounds, to be cast in England. Pennsylvanians called it the Old State House Bell or the Old Independence Bell. The first time the great bell rang, in 1753, it cracked. It was melted down and recast twice in Philadelphia, the second time because the first recast bell didn't have a pleasing tone.

The bell is about four feet tall. Its inscription, "Proclaim Liberty throughout all the land unto all the inhabitants thereof," echoes biblical Leviticus 25:10.

When British troops captured Philadelphia in September 1777, that bell and all the other bells in Philadelphia were spirited out of town so that the British wouldn't melt them down to make cannons. After the war, Philadelphians brought the bell back to the city. They rang it many times to mark important events and anniversaries. The bell cracked again, on July 8, 1835, while tolling with muffled clapper for the funeral parade of U. S. Chief Justice John Marshall.

The bell didn't become a national icon until later. The first documented use of the term "Liberty Bell" appeared in 1839, in a poem published by William Lloyd Garrison in his anti-slavery magazine, *The Liberator*. He pointed out that the bell did not, in fact, proclaim liberty to *all* in the land.

Now fractured beyond repair, the Liberty Bell is no longer rung, but it is tapped with a rubber mallet on special occasions. For example, during World War II, when Allied forces landed on the beaches of Normandy, France, on June 6, 1944, Philadelphia officials tapped the bell to announce D-Day, the invasion of Europe, and the tone was broadcast to all parts of the nation.

Today the bell hangs in a glass-enclosed structure, Liberty Bell Pavilion, just north of Independence Hall in Philadelphia.
    You can see it at:
    https://www.nps.gov/inde/photosmultimedia-soundofthelibertybell.htm

★ Uncle Sam may have originated in a reference to Samuel

Wilson, who sold beef to the U.S. Army during the War of 1812, although most historians think this is unlikely. The first formal mention of Uncle Sam came in 1816 in a book titled *The Adventures of Uncle Sam*.

A similar patriotic figure, Columbia, was the female personification of the country. She first appeared in 1776, but started fading in popularity by the 1920s. Lady Liberty took her place in the popular imagination.

J.M. Flagg painted the most famous representation of Uncle Sam for the cover of *Leslie's Weekly* of July 6, 1916. The painting was used to create the famous recruiting poster, prominent in both world wars, that shows Uncle Sam pointing his finger at the viewer and insisting, "I Want You for U.S. Army."

★ The bald eagle was proposed as the national bird, but Benjamin Franklin thought the wild turkey was "much more respectable," although, he didn't formally propose it for that position. In a letter to his daughter in 1784, after the bald eagle was included in the design of the Great Seal of the United States, he complained that the eagle was "a bird of bad moral character" because it stole food from other birds. The turkey is, "in comparison, a much more respectable bird . . . though a little vain & silly, a bird of Courage." In a letter to a magazine in 1775, Franklin puts forth a case for adopting the rattlesnake as the symbol of the U.S. He wrote that the rattlesnake, unique to America, was a symbol of "wisdom, vigilance, magnanimity, and true courage."

★ The Great Seal of the United States, adopted on June 20, 1782, uses the same red, white, and blue as the American flag. The red on the Great Seal signifies hardiness and valor; the white purity and innocence; and the blue vigilance, perseverance, and justice.

The design on the front or obverse is the coat of arms of the United States. A bald eagle with its wings outstretched supports a shield. In its beak the eagle clutches a scroll with the motto *E pluribus unum* [Out of Many, One]. It holds a bundle of thirteen arrows in its left talon and an olive branch with thirteen leaves and thirteen olives in its right. The eagle's head is turned toward the olive branch, indicating that the United States prefers peace but will always be ready for war.

The back or reverse includes the Eye of Providence, also known as the all-seeing eye, the symbol of God's benevolent oversight. Above the eye are the words *Annuit Coeptis* [He Has Favored Our Undertaking]. Below it is an unfinished pyramid of thirteen steps. It's unfinished, showing the country's potential for growth. MDCCLXXVI [1776] is carved at the base, and below that is the motto *Novus Ordo Seclorum* [A New Order of the Ages].

★ The Democratic Donkey vs the Republican Elephant: Thomas Nast (1840-1902), perhaps the most famous political cartoonist in our history, was responsible for the popularity of two party animals. Nast made a donkey the recognized symbol of the Democratic Party when one of his cartoons appeared in *Harper's Weekly* in 1870. Four years later, in the same magazine, Nast drew a donkey clothed in lion's skin, scaring away all the other animals at the zoo, including the elephant which he labeled "The Republican Vote." That's all it took for the elephant to become associated with Republicans.

We have other national symbols that we don't hear so much about, but they are official based on acts of Congress or presidential proclamations. Our national mammal is the American Bison. Our national bird is the wild turkey. (The bald eagle is our national emblem, but not our national bird.) The oak is our national tree and the rose our national floral emblem, and those plants and others are serviced by our national insect/pollinator, the honeybee.

CHAPTER 12
SCULPTED ICONS

It is still Liberty's torch that we must keep alight,
her vision of justice and enlightenment
that we must always uphold.
LYNDON B. JOHNSON, *36th president*

S ince ancient times, sculpture has been one of humanity's most powerful forms of art. Whether carved from stone, cast in bronze, or molded from clay, sculptures have the ability to move people in profound ways. The three-dimensional, physical nature sculpture gives it a visceral and tangible presence that paintings and other two-dimensional artworks cannot match. The United States is home to many famous and influential sculptural works that have become deeply embedded in our national identity.

★ The Statue of Liberty Enlightening the World was a gift of friendship from the people of France to the people of the United States. This towering neoclassical sculpture commemorates the alliance between the two nations during the Revolutionary War and the freeing of enslaved people after the Civil War. It's a universal symbol of freedom and democracy. Sculpted by Frederic Auguste Bartholdi, the seven rays on Liberty's crown represent the sun, the seven seas, and the seven continents. She cradles in her left arm a tablet that reads, "JULY IV MDCCLXXVI." She strides forward into the future leaving a broken shackle and chain at her feet.

An iron framework designed by Alexandre Gustave Eiffel, the engineer who later designed the Eiffel Tower, supports 3/32-of-an-inch copper skin.

In 1876, Liberty's arm and torch and her head were the first parts constructed in France. The arm was displayed first in Philadelphia and then in New York for several years starting in 1876, before it was returned to France.

The entire statue arrived in the U.S. in 1885 aboard the French freighter *Isere* as 350 individual pieces packed in 214 crates. With a height of more than 151 feet and a waist thirty-five feet thick, she may be the most massive woman in America. On her pedestal, the entire Statue of Liberty reaches 305 feet, which made her the tallest structure in the United States when she gained her place.

Lady Liberty was dedicated on October 28, 1886, designated as a national monument in 1924, and restored for her centennial on July 4, 1986. She stands on Liberty Island (formerly Bedloe's Island) in New York Harbor.

A bronze plaque inside the base displays the Emma Lazarus poem "The New Colossus," written in 1883, with its eternally luminous line: "Give me your tired, your poor, your huddled masses yearning to breathe free":

Not like the brazen giant of Greek fame,
With conquering limbs astride from land to land;
Here at our sea-washed, sunset gates shall stand
A mighty woman with a torch, whose flame
Is the imprisoned lightning, and her name
Mother of Exiles. From her beacon-hand

Glows world-wide welcome; her mild eyes command
The air-bridged harbor that twin cities frame.
"Keep, ancient lands, your storied pomp!" cries she
With silent lips. "Give me your tired, your poor,
Your huddled masses yearning to breathe free,
The wretched refuse of your teeming shore.
Send these, the homeless, tempest-tost to me.
I lift my lamp beside the golden door!"

★ The sixty-foot-high heads of Presidents George Washington (completed 1934), Thomas Jefferson (1936), Theodore Roosevelt (1939), and Abraham Lincoln (1937) appear on 5,725-foot-high Mount Rushmore in the Black Hills of South Dakota. The massive sculpture, titled *Shrine of Democracy,* is included as part of the Mount Rushmore National Memorial. It represents the nation's founding, growth, development, and preservation.

Sculptor Gutzon Borglum (1867-1941) directed four hundred workers in the creation of the monument from 1927 until his death. His son, Lincoln, completed the project a few months later.

In 1937, a grassroots campaign emerged to add another face to Mount Rushmore: women's rights activist, Susan B. Anthony. But with money scarce during the Great Depression, Congress decided that only the four heads already in progress would continue. The original concept was to show the four presidents from the waist up, but ultimately there wasn't enough money to complete that design. Only George Washington has any detail below the neck. Since then, engineers have judged that the surface is inadequate to support another sculpture. Still, names are suggested from time to time. The most recent nominees include Presidents Reagan, Obama, and Trump.

The sculptures were created on land owned by the Sioux Nation under the 1868 Treaty of Fort Laramie. In 1876, after the Battle of the Little Bighorn, the government took the land illegally. The Sioux wanted it back and sued in 1920. In 1980, the Supreme Court awarded the Sioux $102 million compensation. The Sioux refused the judgment; they continue to want their land back. Meanwhile, the judgment has been accruing interest. It's now over a billion dollars.

★ A statue of our sixteenth president, Abraham Lincoln, was erected in 1868, three years after his assassination, in front of the District of Columbia Court of Appeals. The Lincoln Memorial that we know today was not proposed until 1901 and finally authorized in 1910. Construction started in 1914, and it was dedicated in 1922.

During the period when the memorial was authorized and built, a number of organizations in the southern states started erecting statues of Confederate heroes. They were presenting a counter-narrative about the Civil War, which they dubbed "The Lost Cause." Although the shooting may have stopped, the battle of ideas continues to this day.

The marble memorial is in the form of a Greek neoclassical temple. A nineteen-foot statue of a seated Lincoln occupies the center. The temple sits at the west end of a long reflecting pool on the National Mall. At the other end of the pool are the Vietnam Veterans Memorial, the Washington Monument, and the Capitol.

Memorials may seem like static tourist attractions, but they have a living presence. The Lincoln Memorial has been the site of several important milestones in the struggle for equal rights in America, an ongoing part of the battle that started with the first slaves brought to America in 1619.

On April 9, 1939, African American contralto Marian Anderson performed there for audience of 75,000 as well as a nationwide radio audience. She had previously refused the use of Constitution Hall, a venue owned by the Daughters of the American Revolution because the audience would be segregated. First Lady Eleanor Roosevelt suggested the new venue and at the same time publicly resigned her DAR membership.

In 1947, Harry Truman became the first American president to address the National Association for the Advancement of Colored People. He stood on the steps of the Lincoln Memorial. That speech was also broadcast nationally. Truman talked about the need for comprehensive civil rights legislation.

In 1963, a quarter million people joined the March on Washington for Jobs and Freedom. Martin Luther King Jr. stood on the steps of the monument and delivered his "I have a dream" speech. That rally was one of the factors in the passing of the Civil Rights Act of 1964, which outlawed discrimination based on race, color, religion, gender, or national origin. In 1983, another rally marked the twentieth anniversary of that speech and the ideas it espoused, and in 2003, the spot where King stood was engraved to mark the fortieth anniversary.

★ A separate Martin Luther King Jr. Memorial was dedicated in 2011, forty-two years after his assassination in

1968. Called "The Stone of Hope," the thirty-foot-high monument shows King emerging from a block of granite. The title is a reference to a quotation from his "I Have a Dream" speech, which many consider to be one of the greatest examples of American oratory. The full quotation is "Out of a mountain of despair, a stone of hope."

The memorial sits on four acres adjacent to the National Mall. It's one of many monuments to the inspirational leader who used nonviolent resistance and civil disobedience to dismantle legal racial discrimination. The causes he championed were the right to vote, civil rights, labor rights, desegregation, the fight against poverty, and the fight for the end of the Vietnam War. He received the Nobel Peace Prize in 1964 for his work.

PART III
LAND OF THE FREE

Those who deny freedom to others
deserve it not for themselves.
ABRAHAM LINCOLN, *16th president*

CHAPTER 13
THE BATTLE FOR ABOLITION

No man can put a chain
about the ankle of his fellow man
without at last finding the other end
fastened around his own neck.
FREDERICK DOUGLASS, *author and abolitionist*

The opening sentence of our Declaration of Independence states, "We hold these truths to be self-evident, that all men are created equal, that they are endowed by their Creator with certain unalienable Rights, that among these are Life, Liberty and the pursuit of Happiness."

That sentence has been a challenge to Americans ever since it was written.

Estimates vary among historians, but there were at least 450,000 and 500,000 slaves in the thirteen colonies in 1776. The first official census of the new United States took place in 1790. It counted 697,697 slaves out of a total population of 3,929,214. Slaves comprised around 18% of the total U.S. population.

Figures take on even more meaning when you look at them in context. The census showed that in New England, slaves were only 1-2% of the population. Farms there were generally smaller than the plantations in the south, and the crops they grew were not as labor intensive, so there was less demand for farm labor than in the South. In the Middle Colonies like New York and New Jersey, slaves were around 6-8% of the population. In the Southern states, the percentages ranged from 16% in Maryland to over 40% in South Carolina.

The census of 1860, on the eve of the Civil War, showed that those numbers had grown to 3,953,760 enslaved people in a total population of 31,443,321. Now, enslaved people accounted for 8% of the American population.

Article 1, Section 2, Paragraph 3 of the U.S. Constitution reads "Representatives and direct Taxes shall be apportioned among the several states which may be included within this Union, according to their respective Numbers, including those bound to Service for a Term of Years, and excluding Indians not taxed, three fifths of all other persons."

When it came to counting population for the purpose of apportioning representation in the Congress, the northern states had wanted to count only free people. The South had wanted to count everyone, free or enslaved. Since there was a small population of enslaved people in the North and a large population in the South, counting all people would give the South more tax revenue and representatives in the government and thus more power than counting only free people would. The "Three Fifths Compromise" allowed the South representation for three fifths of their slave population.

The Constitution had other articles that touched on the issue of slavery. For example, Article 1 Section 9 limited Congress's power to prohibit the importation of slaves before 1808. Article 4, Section 2 required all states to return fugitive slaves to their owners.

Twelve of our first eighteen presidents owned slaves:

1. George Washington owned between 250 and 600 slaves at different times. His widow, Martha, freed them a year after his death.
2. John Adams opposed slavery and did not own slaves.
3. Thomas Jefferson owned between two hundred and six hundred slaves.
4. James Madison owned more than one hundred slaves.
5. James Monroe owned seventy-five slaves.
6. John Quincy Adams opposed slavery and owned no slaves.
7. Andrew Jackson owned two hundred slaves.
8. Martin Van Buren owned one slave.
9. William Henry Harrison owned eleven slaves.
10. John Tyler owned twenty-nine slaves.
11. James K. Polk owned fifty-nine slaves.
12. Zachary Taylor owned three hundred slaves.
13. Millard Fillmore had no slaves.
14. Franklin Pierce approved of slavery but had no slaves.
15. James Buchanan had no slaves.
16. Abraham Lincoln, president during the Civil War, had no slaves.
17. Andrew Johnson owned nine slaves. He freed them in 1863 during the Civil War.
18. Ulysses S. Grant owned one slave, William Jones. He received Jones as a gift in 1859 and soon afterwards freed him.

In the 1830 census, in a total population of just over 13.1 million, there were 10,537,378 Whites, 2,328,642 slaves, and 319,599 free Blacks. That year the census started counting slave owners. You may be surprised to read that out of 105,635 slave owners in America, 3,778 were free Blacks. (Native Americans also owned slaves but neither Native Americans nor their slaves were counted in the census.)

It's easy from our modern viewpoint to look back on those presidents and other slave owners and call them misguided or even evil, but they were living by the morals and ethics of their time. Before we judge them harshly, we should consider how our descendants will judge us about how we handle the controversial questions of our time.

During the antebellum period (1815-1861), between the War of 1812 and the Civil War, the country expanded from eighteen states to thirty-four. Each slave state admitted increased the power and influence of the Southern states; each free state increased the power of the North. As each state was admitted, debate about whether that state would be slave or free took place, and those debates were not always peaceful. For example, Kansas earned the nickname "Bloody Kansas" in the 1850s because of the pitched battles between "Free-Staters" and pro-slavery factions. Hundreds were killed. Seemingly irreconcilable tensions between the two sections of the country continued to grow.

Gradually the movement for abolition also grew as individuals and groups began speaking up against slavery.

One of the earliest documented public expressions against slavery in what became the United States dates back to 1688. In that year, German Quakers living in the Germantown settlement in Pennsylvania wrote a protest against the practice of slavery and sent it to their governing body. The Germantown Quaker "Petition Against Slavery" is considered the earliest public condemnation of slavery in the colonies.

It cited the biblical admonition to "do unto others as you would have them do unto you," and urged readers "to have a considerable inspection and weight on the matter . . . to do what is reasonable towards the stopping of this lamentable practice of making slaves of the Negroes."

Other public opposition to slavery appeared in 1701, when Puritans in Massachusetts opposed the practice with a petition.

As ideas about abolition began to be debated, slaves were not passive. During the seventeenth, eighteenth, and nineteenth centuries slave rebellions were not uncommon. Of the more than 250 rebellions during that time involving ten or more slaves, probably the most famous was that of Nat Turner in 1831. The rebellion was put down and Turner hanged, but that did not mitigate fear about a possible "next" uprising.

Opposition to slavery grew and leaders emerged:

★   Frederick Douglass (1818?-1895) escaped from his slave master in 1838. Three years later, he spoke eloquently about freedom at a meeting of the Massachusetts Antislavery Society, which immediately hired him to travel and lecture about being a slave. In 1845, Douglass published his autobiography, *Narrative of the Life of Frederick Douglass, An American Slave*. Fearing capture when the book was released, he fled to England and Ireland, where he earned enough money to return to the United States in 1847 in order to buy his freedom. He founded an antislavery newspaper, the *North Star*, in Rochester, New York, and continued to speak and work against slavery and discrimination. During the Civil War, Douglass helped recruit African Americans for the Union Army and consulted several times with President Lincoln. After the war, he worked to gain civil rights for former slaves. He also supported the cause of women's suffrage.

★ William Lloyd Garrison (1805–1879) was one of America's most active abolitionists. He was publisher of the abolitionist newspaper the *Liberator*, published 1831-1865, and a founder of the American Anti-Slavery Society. He worked his whole life to end slavery and saw his goal realized at the end of the Civil War. Later he became a prominent leader of the women's suffrage movement.

★ The Grimké sisters, Sarah (1792-1893) and Angelina 1805-1879) were born on a plantation in South Carolina and grew up in a family that owned hundreds of slaves. In her twenties, Sarah moved to Philadelphia where she lived for several years and converted to Quakerism. Later, her sister lived there with her, and the two women formed a strong commitment to abolition. They became powerful public speakers and writers for the cause. They were among the first women in America to take on such a public role and were criticized from church pulpits for not being silent and submissive, as women were expected to be. That caused them to understand the link between slaves' rights to freedom and women's rights. Their life-long commitment to women's rights became as strong as their commitment to abolition.

★ Sojourner Truth (1797-1883) was born Isabella Baumfree, a slave in Ulster County, New York, and was freed in 1827, when New York outlawed slavery. Taking the name Sojourner Truth, she became an evangelist and social reformer preaching for abolition and women's rights. She helped many escaped slaves. In 1864, she visited President Abraham Lincoln in the White House. She also received many posthumous honors.

★ Born a slave, Harriet Tubman (1820?-1913) escaped in 1849 and went to Philadelphia. In 1850, she made the first of nineteen trips south to help more than three hundred slaves, including her parents, escape via the Underground Railroad. These trips put Tubman in danger. If she had been captured, she could have been enslaved again, or she could have been prosecuted under the federal Fugitive Slave Act, which made it a crime to aid a runaway slave.

★ Dred Scott (1795–1858) was a slave who sued in Missouri for his freedom and that of his wife, Harriet, and two daughters, Eliza and Lizzie, arguing that they had lived with their masters in Illinois and Wisconsin Territory, where slavery was illegal, and were therefore free. In 1857, by a 7–2 majority, the Supreme Court ruled that Black African Americans were not citizens and had no rights or privileges under the Constitution, so a slave had no right to bring suit. The decision deepened sectional tensions and is still considered the worst decision the Supreme Court ever made. Scott and his family were later freed.

★ Levi (1798-1877) and Catherine Coffin (1803-1881), Quakers in Fountain City, Indiana, welcomed and helped more than three thousand slaves on their way to freedom in northern states and Canada via the Underground Railroad between 1847 and 1857. Levi was sometimes called the "President of the Underground Railroad" and the Coffin home earned the name "Grand Central Station." The railroad, organized in the 1830s and running through the Civil War, was a series of secret routes and safe houses that stretched from the deep south to Canada. Guides, called "conductors," led escaping slaves to freedom at the risk of their own lives. One estimate suggests that more than one hundred thousand slaves found freedom that way.

★ Militant abolitionist John Brown (1800–1859) and twenty-one followers attacked and occupied an armory building at Harpers Ferry, Virginia, between October 16 and October 18, 1859. Brown had earned his reputation as a dangerous militant in the battles in "Bloody Kansas." He was convinced that slaves all over the South would rise up and join him. Marines under the command of Colonel Robert E. Lee (later, General Lee, leader of the southern Confederate forces) stormed the building and killed ten attackers. Six townspeople and two marines also died, and a number of people were injured in the gun battle. Brown was tried and hanged on December 2, 1859. His actions, considered a failure at first glance, galvanized the already polarized discussion about slavery and probably hastened the beginning of the Civil War.

★ Freed and escaped enslaved people also wrote books detailing the cruelty of slavery. Possibly the best known of these slave narratives is *Incidents in the Life of a Slave Girl,* by Harriet Jacobs, writing as Linda Brent. In this 1861 book, Jacobs detailed the sexual indignities in the lives of enslaved females and the pain of raising children who might be sold at any moment. She escaped slavery by hiding for seven years in a tiny three-foot high crawlspace attic in her grandmother's house. She could hear her children talking below, but never dared contact them for fear that they might accidentally expose her. She finally made her way to New York City.

Other slave narratives include *The Narrative of the Life of Frederick Douglass, an American Slave; The Narrative of William W. Brown, a Fugitive Slave; The Life of Olaudah Equiano; The Narrative of Sojourner Truth; Twelve Years Slave* by Solomon Northup; *Narrative of the life of Henry Box Brown;* and *A Narrative of the Adventures Escape of Moses Roper.*

★ Harriet Beecher Stowe (1811-1896) published more than forty books in her lifetime. She and her husband, Calvin Ellis Stowe, were ardent abolitionists. They participated in the Underground Railroad, hiding fugitive slaves in their home in Maine during the transit to Canada. Her most famous book, *Uncle Tom's Cabin*, published in 1852, shone a searing light on the cruelty of slavery. It sold more than three hundred thousand copies in the U.S. the first year and over two hundred thousand in Great Britain. Millions read it. It was second, after the Bible, in sales in the U.S. during the nineteenth century and is still in print. *Uncle Tom's Cabin* rallied abolitionist sentiment in both America and Great Britain in the pre-Civil War era. When Stowe visited Abraham Lincoln in the White House in 1862, he said, "So this is the little lady who made this big war."

Many other names, such as William Still (1821-1902), Thomas Garrett (1789-1871), David Walker (1785-1830), and Theodore Weld (1803-1895), can be added to this list as abolitionists shifted from philosophy and debate to activism. Tension between the North and South continued to rise.

The abolition of slavery was a crucial milestone in America living up to its founding ideals of human equality. However, the struggle for true racial equality and justice was far from over, as Black Americans continued to face oppression, discrimination, and denial of rights in the decades following emancipation. But the abolitionist movement ultimately succeeded in righting one of America's greatest moral wrongs and set the stage for further progress in civil rights.

CHAPTER 14
ABRAHAM LINCOLN'S
GETTYSBURG ADDRESS

His words had the wisdom of ages
and the force of thunder.
With Lincoln, we glimpsed where we might go.
Haven't his words helped guide
the holding of this country together,
the realization of that noble dream
that insists all of us are created equal?
BARACK OBAMA, *44th president*

Almost eight decades after the end of the Revolutionary
War (1783), there erupted another war (1861-1865). It
was called the War Between the States, the War against North-
ern Aggression, Mr. Lincoln's War, the War for the Union, the
War for Abolition, the War for Separation, the War for States'
Rights, the War for Southern Independence, and the Civil War.

Mostly known today as the Civil War, the conflict seared
our national consciousness and forever changed what it means
to be an American.

At dawn of July 1, 1863, the war had been unfolding for
more than two years. For the next three days in the Battle of
Gettysburg, Pennsylvania, Americans slew Americans in the
most lethal battle ever fought on United States soil. In that most
pivotal clash of the Civil War, more than 51,000 soldiers were
killed, wounded, or reported missing.

Four and a half months later, on November 19, 1863, a
crowd of about fifteen thousand gathered at Gettysburg to consecrate a new Civil War cemetery. The story's headline in *The*

New York Times makes clear who was the designated speaker of the day:

IMMENSE NUMBERS OF VISITORS
Oration By Hon. Edward Everett
Speeches of President Lincoln,
Mr. Seward and Governor Seymour

Most of us are unaware that the nation's most celebrated orator, Edward Everett of Massachusetts, delivered the main address that Thursday afternoon. The speech that Lincoln gave was listed as "Dedicatory Remarks by the President of the United States." Those remarks were intended as a brief and formal follow-up to Everett's two-hour oration dedicating the opening of the Soldiers' National Cemetery at Gettysburg.

What happened at Gettysburg was that with 271 fateful words in but ten sentences, Abraham Lincoln forged "a new birth of freedom" out of blood and shock. Within the brief compass of less than three minutes, he gave a young nation a voice to sing of itself:

Four score and seven years ago our fathers brought forth on this continent a new nation, conceived in Liberty, and dedicated to the proposition that all men are created equal.

Now we are engaged in a great civil war, testing whether that nation or any nation so conceived and so dedicated, can long endure. We are met on a great battle-field of that war. We have come to dedicate a portion of that field, as a final resting place for those who here gave their lives that that nation might live. It is altogether fitting and proper that we should do this.

But, in a larger sense, we can not dedicate — we can not consecrate — we can not hallow — this ground. The brave men, living and dead, who struggled here, have consecrated it, far above our poor power to add or detract. The world will little note, nor long remember what we say here, but it can never forget what they did here. It is for us the living, rather, to be dedicated here to the unfinished work which they who fought here have thus far so nobly advanced. It is rather for us to be here dedicated to the great task remaining before us — that from these honored dead we take increased devotion to that cause for which they gave the last full measure of devotion — that we here highly resolve that these dead shall not have died in vain —that this nation, under God, shall have a new birth of freedom — and that government of the people, by the people, for the people, shall not perish from the earth.

Afterward, Edward Everett took Lincoln aside and said, "My speech will soon be forgotten; yours never will. How gladly would I exchange my hundred pages for your twenty lines!" The very brevity of Lincoln's text rendered it more luminous, universal, and memorable. That compactness allowed hundreds of newspapers to print the text and countless school-children to memorize it. More than eight score years ago, on that brisk, sunny day in Pennsylvania, a weary president said, "The world will little note, nor long remember what we say here." In that he was mistaken. The world noted and has never ceased remembering. Abraham Lincoln had forged not only a creed of democracy, but also, in the words of poet Carl Sandburg, "the great American poem."

CHAPTER 15
CIVIL RIGHTS

I am sick and tired of being sick and tired.
FANNY LOU HAMER, *civil rights activist*

The Thirteenth Amendment, adopted on December 6, 1865, abolished slavery throughout the United States. The Fourteenth Amendment (1868) defined citizenship for the first time and included former slaves. The Fifteenth Amendment (1870) prohibited denying a citizen the right to vote based on "race, color, or previous condition of servitude."

These words ring out from the Emancipation Proclamation and took effect on January 1, 1863. The proclamation freed all the slaves in the ten remaining rebellious states, 3.1 million of the 4 million slaves in the United States.

In 1896, the Supreme Court justices, in a vote of 7–1, upheld the doctrine of "separate but equal," legalizing segregation and Jim Crow laws in the United States. In Plessy v. Ferguson, the justices reasoned that, as long as the facilities for each race were equal in quality, racial segregation laws did not violate the U.S. Constitution. The decision legitimized the many state laws re-establishing the racially segregating Jim Crow laws that had been passed in the American South after the end of the Reconstruction era in 1877.

Plessy v. Ferguson stood until May 17, 1954, when the Supreme Court issued one its most consequential decisions. The case was Brown v. Board of Education of Topeka, and the unanimous ruling overturned the "separate but equal" doctrine.

Attorney Thurgood Marshall worked for the National Association for the Advancement of Colored People (NAACP) from 1936 to 1961. He represented the NAACP before the Supreme Court in 1954 in *Brown vs. Board of Education of Topeka*.

He argued that "separate but equal" was unconstitutional under the Fourteenth Amendment, and the Court agreed with him unanimously. That decision ended racial segregation in the public schools of America. President Lyndon Johnson appointed Marshall to the Supreme Court. The first African American justice, Thurgood Marshall served from 1967 until his retirement in 1991.

The ramifications of Brown rippled across American society, lending vital moral legitimacy to the burgeoning Civil Rights Movement. It inspired principled resistance like the Montgomery bus boycott and grassroots activism that ultimately led to dismantling segregation and achieving milestones like the Civil Rights Act and Voting Rights Act in the 1960s.

The Supreme Court's unanimous ruling in Brown v. Board of Education of Topeka marked a pivotal turning point in America's journey toward racial equality and justice under the law. While the path has been long and difficult, Brown articulated a profoundly moral and democratic vision of an integrated society free of legally codified discrimination that continues to inspire the ongoing struggle for civil rights.

★ Booker T. Washington (1856-1915) lived the first nine years of his life as a slave. He went on to found Tuskegee Institute (now Tuskegee University), and founded the National Negro Business League with the help of Andrew Carnegie. He became the leading voice for a generation of former slaves and their descendants. He advised Presidents Theodore Roosevelt and William Howard Taft.

★ Scholar and activist William Edward Burghardt Du Bois, better known as W.E.B. Du Bois (1868-1963), was the first African American to earn a Ph.D. from Harvard University 1895. He wrote prolifically, including *The Souls of Black Folk,* and was the best-known spokesperson for African American rights during the first half of the twentieth century. In 1909, Du Bois co-founded the National Association for the Advancement of Colored People (NAACP).

★ In 1955, Rosa Parks (1913-2005), an African American civil rights activist, refused to give up her seat on a public bus to a White man in Montgomery, Alabama. She was arrested for refusing to move to the back of the bus and was fined fourteen dollars. Her act of civil disobedience sparked the Montgomery Bus Boycott, led by Martin Luther King Jr. Blacks in Montgomery boycotted buses for more than a year. In 1956, the U.S. Supreme Court declared segregated seating on the city's buses unconstitutional. The boycott ended, but its success encouraged other protests demanding civil rights for Blacks.

★ Martin Luther King Jr. (1929-1968), an African American Baptist minister, was a leader of the civil rights movement from 1955 until his assassination in 1968, when he was just thirty-nine years of age. He was instrumental in establishing the Southern Christian Leadership Conference, which promoted nonviolent demonstrations to protest racial discrimination. A powerful and charismatic orator, King, from the steps of the Lincoln Memorial on August 28, 1963, delivered his "I Have a Dream" speech to more than 220,000 civil rights supporters. Many scholars rank that oration as the most important American speech of the twentieth century. His efforts helped lead to the passing of the Civil Rights Act of 1964 and the Voting Rights Act of 1965. He received the 1964 Nobel Peace Prize.

★ Barack Obama (1961–) was our forty-fourth president, the first of African American descent. His father, Barack Obama Sr., was a Luo from Nyang'oma Kogelo, Kenya. Before Obama, there were many other notable Black men and women who sought the presidency as Republican or Democratic candidates. They include Shirley Chisholm, Jesse Jackson, Alan Keyes, Carol Moseley Braun, and Al Sharpton.

President Obama's signature legislative achievement was the Patient Protection and Affordable Care Act, also known as "Obamacare," passed on March 23, 2010. The act was designed to ensure access to affordable health insurance for all Americans.

CHAPTER 16
FEMALE STRONG

No country can ever truly flourish
if it stifles the potential of its women
and deprives itself
of the contributions of half its citizens.
MICHELLE OBAMA, *author and First Lady*

From the American Revolution to the present day, women have battled to secure the same political, economic, and social rights as men. The women's suffrage movement was a decades-long struggle to win the right for women to vote in the United States.

The aftermath of the Civil War infused that movement with additional energy. In 1870, Black men achieved the vote, but a half century elapsed before the suffrage movement reached its goal. That happened on August 28, 1920, with the ratification of the Nineteenth Amendment, which proclaims "The right of citizens of the United States to vote shall not be denied or abridged by the United States or by any State on account of sex." The journey toward women's enfranchisement was long and arduous and pioneered by determined activists known as suffragettes. Some suffragettes endured fines, forced feeding, beatings, and imprisonment, including solitary confinement.

★ Elizabeth Cady Stanton (1815-1902) led the early battle for women's suffrage and for the abolition of slavery. She and Lucretia Mott (1793-1880) organized the 1848 Seneca Falls Convention, the nation's first women's rights meeting. The convention, passed a resolution in favor of women's suffrage despite opposition from some of its organizers, who believed the idea was too extreme.

In 1869, Stanton and Susan B. Anthony (1820-1906) founded the National Woman Suffrage Association, for which she served as president for more than thirty years.

★ One of the most influential early suffragettes was Susan B. Anthony (1820-1902). Along with Elizabeth Cady Stanton, Anthony founded the National Woman Suffrage Association in 1869. She dedicated over fifty years of her life to the women's suffrage cause through writings, speeches, petitions, and an arrest for illegally voting in the 1872 presidential election. Anthony played a pivotal role in paving the path for the Nineteenth Amendment.

★ Ida B. Wells (1862-1931) was an African American investigative journalist who fought for voting rights and against racial injustice. In the 1890s, she led an anti-lynching crusade. As a co-founder of the National Association for the Advancement of Colored People (NAACP), Wells advocated for the rights of both women and African Americans, understanding the intersectionality of these causes. Her courageous reporting and speeches challenged the racist status quo.

★ Carrie Chapman Catt (1859-1947) re-invigorated the stagnant women's suffrage movement in the early 1900s as a skilled activist and organizer. Succeeding Susan B. Anthony as the president of the National American Woman Suffrage Association, Catt trained women for direct political action to get women's suffrage added to the national party platforms. After the Nineteenth Amendment was adopted, Catt reorganized the Suffrage Association into the League of Women Voters.

★ On the radical front was Quaker suffragette Alice Paul (1885-1977), the leader of the more militant National Woman's Party. Paul embraced civil disobedience tactics like hunger strikes, massive protests, picketing the White House and silently carrying signs bearing messages such as "Mr. President, how long must women wait for liberty?" which drew widespread backlash from authorities. At the same time, Paul's confrontational methods earned substantial publicity for the suffragist cause.

The tireless efforts of these determined leaders, along with countless other women (and men) devoted to the movement, paved the way for the Nineteenth Amendment. Their tireless efforts to expand democracy and secure voting rights for women were finally realized when the Nineteenth Amendment was ratified in 1920, marking a monumental achievement for equality and justice for all Americans.

PART IV
HAIL TO THE CHIEFS

When you get to be president,
Here are the honors, the twenty-one-gun salutes —
all those things. You have to remember
it isn't for you. It's for the presidency.
HARRY S. TRUMAN, *33rd president*

CHAPTER 17
A PROCESSION OF PRESIDENTS

The presidency has made every man who occupied it,
no matter how small, bigger than he was;
and no matter how big, not big enough for its demands.
LYNDON B. JOHNSON, 36th *president*

When George Washington became president in 1789, other national leaders included the King of France, the Czarina of Russia, the Emperor of China, and the Shogun of Japan. Today, no king rules France, no czar rules Russia, no emperor rules China, and no shogun rules Japan. But the office of president of the United States endures and prevails.

Very few nations have a governmental system that allows any ordinary citizen to become the leader of the country. But we do. Thomas Jefferson was our third president, Richard Nixon our thirty-seventh, and Harry Truman our thirty-third. That proves that any Tom, Dick, and Harry can become president of the United States.

Our presidents have been movie-star handsome — Ronald Reagan was, in fact, a movie star. On the other hand, the New York Herald described Abraham Lincoln thusly: "Lincoln is the leanest, lankiest, most ungainly mass of legs, arms, and hatchet-face ever strung upon a single frame. He has most unwarrantably abused the privilege which all politicians have of being ugly." Lincoln was known to make fun of his legendary homeliness and gangly height. During one of their 1858 debates when they were running for the Senate, Stephen Douglas accused Abraham Lincoln of being two-faced. Replied Lincoln calmly,

"I leave it to my audience: If I had two faces, would I be wearing this one?"

They have been rolling in dough and dirt poor. George Washington's net worth was over 700 million in today's dollars and Harry Truman's under one million.

They have been highly educated and barely schooled. Woodrow Wilson earned a Ph.D. in Political Science from Johns Hopkins University, while Andrew Johnson never attended school but trained as a tailor and wore only suits that he himself had made.

As we begin our exploration of America's chief executives, let's review the names and terms in office of the men (we're still awaiting a woman) who have been president of the United States:

1. George Washington, 1789-1797
2. John Adams, 1797-1801
3. Thomas Jefferson, 1801-1809
4. James Madison, 1809-1817
5. James Monroe, 1817-1825
6. John Quincy Adams, 1825-1829
7. Andrew Jackson, 1829-1837
8. Martin Van Buren, 1837-1841
9. William Henry Harrison, 1841
10. John Tyler, 1841-1845
11. James K. Polk, 1845-1849
12. Zachary Taylor, 1849-1850
13. Millard Fillmore, 1850-1853
14. Franklin Pierce, 1853-1857
15. James Buchanan, 1857-1861
16. Abraham Lincoln, 1861- 1865
17. Andrew Johnson, 1865-1869
18. Ulysses S. Grant, 1869-1877

19. Rutherford B. Hayes, 1877-1881
20. James A. Garfield, 1881
21. Chester A. Arthur, 1881-1885
22. Grover Cleveland, 1885-1889
23. Benjamin Harrison, 1889-1893
24. Grover Cleveland, 1893-1897
25. William McKinley, 1897-1901
26. Theodore Roosevelt, 1901-1909
27. William Howard Taft, 1909-1913
28. Woodrow Wilson, 1913-1921
29. Warren G. Harding, 1921-1923
30. Calvin Coolidge, 1923-1929
31. Herbert Hoover, 1929-1933
32. Franklin D. Roosevelt, 1933-1945
33. Harry S. Truman, 1945-1953
34. Dwight D. Eisenhower,1953-1961
35. John F. Kennedy, 1961- 1963
36. Lyndon B. Johnson, 1963-1969
37. Richard M. Nixon, 1969-1974
38. Gerald Ford, 1974-1977
39. Jimmy Carter, 1977-1981
40. Ronald Reagan, 1981-1989
41. George H.W. Bush, 1989-1993.
42. Bill Clinton, 1993-2001
43. George W. Bush, 2001-2009
44. Barack Obama, 2009-2017
45. Donald Trump, 2017-2021
46. Joe Biden, 2021-

CHAPTER 18
FASCINATING FACTS
ABOUT OUR PRESIDENTS

Americanism is a question of principle,
of purpose, of idealism, of character.
It is not a matter of birthplace,
or creed or line of descent.
THEODORE ROOSEVELT, *26ᵗʰ president*

Historian Henry Adams, the grandson and great-grandson of presidents, wrote that the American president "resembles the commander of a ship at sea. He must have a helm to grasp, a course to steer, a port to seek." Here are some intriguing facts about the voyages that our presidents have steered while captaining the ship of state.

Our second and third presidents, John Adams (age 90) and Thomas Jefferson (age 83), political rivals, then friends, both died on July 4, 1826, exactly fifty years after adoption of the Declaration of Independence.

As Jefferson lay weak and dying in his home in Monticello, Virginia, on the evening of July 3, he whispered, "Is this the Fourth?" To quiet the former president, his personal secretary and grandson-in-law, Nicholas Trist, answered, "Yes." Jefferson fell asleep with a smile. His heart continued to beat until shortly after noon the next day.

At dawn of that day, John Adams was expiring in his home in Quincy, Massachusetts. A servant asked the fading Adams, "Do you know what day it is?" "Oh yes," responded the lion in winter. "It is the glorious Fourth of July." He then lapsed into a stupor but awakened to hear the celebratory firecrackers exploding in the sky. "Thomas Jefferson survives," Adams sighed. He ceased to breathe around sunset, about six hours after Jefferson.

★ At five feet four inches and weighing about a hundred pounds, James Madison was our most compact president. One observer marveled that he had "never seen so much mind in little matter." In fact, Madison is probably our only president who weighed less than his IQ.

★ Abraham Lincoln, at six feet four inches, was our loftiest president, when the average Civil War soldier was five feet seven inches. When asked, "How tall are you?" Lincoln would reply, "Tall enough to reach the ground."

★ In 1912, President William Howard Taft ran as a Republican for re-election against the Democratic nominee, Woodrow Wilson. Former president Theodore Roosevelt said of his successor, "Taft meant well, but he meant well feebly," so Roosevelt also entered the fray, a candidate for the Bull Moose Party. Roosevelt and Taft split the Republican vote, and Wilson with 48 percent of the popular vote won handily. Taft placed third with an abysmal 23 percent of the popular vote, the lowest ever for an incumbent president. Unstintingly good-humored, Taft sighed, "I have one consolation. No one candidate was ever elected ex-president by such a large majority."

★ When President Warren Harding appointed Taft Chief Justice of the Supreme Court in 1921, eight years after his presidency, he became the only man ever to have headed both the executive and judicial branches of our government. Taft swore in both Calvin Coolidge in 1923 and Herbert Hoover in 1929 at their inaugurations.

★ Richard Nixon resigned from the White House on August 9, 1974, the only president to do so. Spiro Agnew, his vice president, had resigned ten months earlier. As a result, Ford was, for two years, the only man who served as both vice president (replacing Agnew) and president (replacing Nixon) without having been elected to either office. The only elected office Ford ever held was a Western Michigan congressional seat. Ford's vice president, Nelson Rockefeller, who had previously served as governor of New York, had never served in national office.

★ Ronald Reagan became president two weeks shy of his seventieth birthday — older than any other president up to that time — and left office two weeks short of his seventy-eighth. At the age of seventy years and seven months, Donald Trump superseded Reagan as the most chronologically endowed man to ascend to the Oval Office. Then, superseding Trump, Joe Biden became president at the age of seventy-eight

★ Our third, fourth, and fifth presidents — Thomas Jefferson, James Madison, and James Monroe — consecutively served two full terms as president for a total of twenty-four years, 1801-1825. It took almost two centuries to repeat that pattern — Bill Clinton, George W. Bush, and Barack Obama, 1993-2017.

CHAPTER 19
TALES OF THE PRESIDENCY

The presidency is not an office for one man
to hold all the power.
It's to represent the people of the United States.
GERALD FORD, *38th president*

T he word *history* descends from the Latin *historia*, meaning
"narrative, tale, story," and the saga of our American presidents is festooned with fascinating stories. Here are a few of
our favorites:

★ In July 1864, the populace of Washington D.C. was ter-
rified. General Robert E. Lee had sent 10,000 Confederate
troops under the command of General Jubal Early to try to take
the city. Journalist Noah Brooks described the scene: "The city is
in a ferment; men are marching to and fro; able-bodied citizens are
gobbled up and put in the District militia; refugees come flying in
from the country, bringing their household goods with them; nobody is permitted to go out on the Maryland roads without a pass."

Fort Stevens, one of forty forts encircling Washington, was five
miles north of the White House in what is now Silver Spring, Maryland. The Battle of Fort Stevens began on July 11. President
Abraham Lincoln understood the significance of this battle. If
Washington fell, that was probably the end of the war. The Confederates would have won. On July 12, as he left the White
House, Lincoln was asked if he was fleeing the Confederates.
He replied, "Oh, no, but there is excitement among our boys,
and I go out to encourage them." He traveled to the front to
inspect Union defenses. He wanted his soldiers to see that he

was with them. As Lincoln stood behind an earthen parapet looking at the Confederate line, a sharpshooter, probably aiming at Lincoln in his stove pipe hat, sent a bullet through the man standing next to him.

It was the only time in American history that a president exposed himself to combat, but Lincoln's physical courage surprised no one. He believed that if someone was determined to kill him, nothing could prevent it. He refused to worry and focused on winning the war.

The Union forces drove off General Early and his army that day in a turning point that led to the end of the war the following year.

★ Ulysses S. Grant claimed to smoke seven to ten cigars a day. When word got out of Grant's love of stogies, people all over the world sent him more than ten thousand boxes of cigars. The result was terminal cancer of the throat. For the last few months of his life, he had to sleep in an easy chair to avoid choking.

During his final months, Grant struggled to complete writing *Personal Memoirs of U.S. Grant*. The autobiography was published by his close friend Mark Twain in 1885, the same year that Twain came out with *The Adventures of Huckleberry Finn*.

Grant died shortly after his memoirs were published. Three hundred thousand copies sold the first year. The book ultimately brought in $450,000 for his wife, Julia, and family, the equivalent of more than fifteen million in today's dollars. It's still in print and remains one of the finest accounts of the Civil War ever written.

★Mothers sewed stuffed bear dolls before President Theodore Roosevelt came along, but no one called them teddy bears. Not until November, 1902, when the president went on a bear hunt in Smedes, Mississippi.

Roosevelt was acting as adjudicator for a border dispute between the states of Louisiana and Mississippi. On November 14, during a break in the negotiations, he was invited by southern friends to go bear hunting. Roosevelt felt that he could consolidate his support in the South by appearing there in the relaxed atmosphere of a hunting party, so he accepted the invitation.

During the hunt, Roosevelt's hosts cornered a bear cub, and a guide roped it to a tree for the president to kill. Roosevelt declined to shoot the cub, believing such an act to be beneath his dignity as a hunter and said "I couldn't be able to look my boys in the face again."

That Sunday's *Washington Post* carried a cartoon, drawn by Clifford Berryman (1869-1949), of President Theodore

Roosevelt. TR stood in hunting gear, rifle in hand and his back turned toward the cowering cub. The caption read, "Drawing the line in Mississippi" referring both to the border dispute and to animal ethics.

Now the story switches to Brooklyn, New York. There Russian immigrants Morris and Rose Michtom owned a candy store where they also sold handmade stuffed animals. Inspired by Berryman's cartoon, Rose Michtom made a toy bear and displayed it in the shop window. The bear proved wildly popular with the public.

The Michtoms sent President Roosevelt the very bear they had put in their window They said it was meant for Roosevelt's grandchildren and asked TR for permission to use his name for the bear. The president replied, "I don't know what my name may mean to the bear business but you're welcome to use it."

Rose and Morris began turning out stuffed cubs labeled *Teddy's bear*, in honor of our twenty-sixth president. As the demand increased, the family hired extra seamstresses and rented a warehouse. Their operation eventually became the Ideal Toy Corporation.

The bear was a prominent emblem in Roosevelt's successful 1904 election campaign, and *Teddy's bear* was enshrined in dictionaries in 1907. Cartoonist Berryman never sought compensation for the many uses of the cub he had created. He simply smiled and said, "I have made thousands of children happy; that is enough for me."

★ Campaigning for the presidency on October 14, 1912, as a candidate for the Bull Moose party, Theodore Roosevelt gave a speech immediately after being struck by a bullet from a would-be assassin. The audience gasped in horror when the former president unbuttoned his vest to reveal his bloodstained shirt. He opened his speech thusly: "Ladies and gentleman, I don't know whether you fully understand that I have just been shot; but it takes more than that to kill a Bull Moose."

He reached into his coat pocket and pulled out a bullet-riddled, fifty-page speech. Holding up his prepared remarks, Roosevelt continued. "Fortunately I had my manuscript, so you see I was going to make a long speech, and there is a bullet — there is where the bullet went through — and it probably saved me from it going into my heart. The bullet is in me now, so I cannot make a very long speech, but I will try my best." Only after completing his speech did TR agree to be taken to a hospital.

★ At the age of thirty-nine, Franklin Roosevelt was paralyzed by polio. He served his entire presidency without the use of his legs but, through rigorous exercise, learned to stand with the help of braces. His wheelchair was designed with no arms to give the appearance of a regular chair. Roosevelt seldom mentioned his polio but once observed, "If you had spent two years in bed trying to wiggle your big toe, after that anything else would seem easy."

★ One of the iconic photos of the twentieth century is a picture of newly elected President Harry Truman, a Democrat, holding up a copy of the *Chicago Daily Tribune*. The look on Truman's face is one of pure joy. The banner headline that made him so happy? DEWEY DEFEATS TRUMAN! Anticipating a victory for Truman's opponent, New York Governor Thomas E. Dewey, the *Tribune*, a Republican-leaning paper printed and distributed 150,000 copies of that issue.

Before the returns came in and based on the assumptions of pundits and pollsters, the editors had assumed that a splinter Democratic party, the Dixiecrats, would act as spoilers and give the race to Dewey. They changed the headline to DEMOCRATS MAKE SWEEP OF STATE OFFICES when they realized their error. An interesting postscript to this story is that the photo was taken two days after the election.

Communication in those days was slow. Truman knew he'd won, but he hadn't seen the paper before that moment.

★ In 1962, John F. Kennedy entertained a group of Nobel Prize winners at the White House. After a short welcoming speech, Kennedy raised his glass to toast the luminaries in the room. "I want to tell you how welcome you are to the White House. I think this is the most extraordinary collection of talent, of human knowledge, that has ever been gathered together at the White House, with the possible exception of when Thomas Jefferson dined alone."

Kennedy may have been reflecting on the fact that, in addition to Jefferson's political acumen, our third president designed many of the first buildings of the University of Virginia, which he founded, and two of his other architectural designs — Monticello and Bremo — are still among the most exquisite country houses in America. He also had much to do with the planning of Washington, D.C., and invented early versions of the swivel chair, collapsible writing table, and pedometer, to measure his walks.

★ Many would label Ronald Reagan as our most television-savvy president. In his 1980 debate with Jimmy Carter, Reagan, at the end of the exchanges, made sure to walk across the dais to shake hands with Carter — to show that Reagan was clearly the taller, and hence the more commanding, of the two. In his 1984 televised presidential debate against his considerably younger opponent, Walter Mondale, Reagan quipped, "I will not make age an issue in this campaign. I am not going to exploit, for political purposes, my opponent's youth and inexperience."

CHAPTER 20
PATTERNS OF THE PRESIDENCY

The increasing power of the presidency
makes the patterns of its history worthy of study.
CLINTON ROSSITER, *Historian*

Seven presidents elected at intervals of twenty years died in office — William Henry Harrison (elected in 1840), Abraham Lincoln (1860), James Garfield (1880), William McKinley (1900), Warren Harding (1920), Franklin Roosevelt (1940), and John F. Kennedy (1960).

First noted in a *Ripley's Believe It or Not* book published in 1934, this string of untimely presidential deaths is variously known as the curse of Tippecanoe, the zero-year curse, and the twenty-year curse. It was also called the Tecumseh's curse, Tecumseh being the chief of the Shawnee Nation defeated by William Henry Harrison at the Battle of Tippecanoe in 1811. Ronald Reagan, elected in 1980 and shot by John Hinckley Jr. on March 30, 1981, almost continued the deadly sequence but survived and broke the pattern.

The more we delve into the lives of our American presidents, the more we see patterns that connect their feats, their fates, and their families:

★ Except for Barack Obama, the publicly acknowledged ancestry of our first forty-five presidents has been limited to seven heritages or some combination thereof — Dutch, English, German, Irish, Scottish, Swiss, and Welsh. Barack Obama was our first president of African heritage, the son of a Kenyan father.

★ Thirty-two of the forty-five men who have been president have been Protestant when in office. Eight have been "Christian or Other," four Unitarian, and two Catholic.

★ A significant number of our presidents have been related. John Adams was the father of John Quincy Adams and George H. W. Bush the father of George W. Bush. William Henry Harrison was the grandfather of Benjamin Harrison. James Madison and Zachary Taylor were second cousins. And genealogists have determined that Franklin Roosevelt was a fifth cousin of Theodore Roosevelt and related to eleven other presidents by blood or marriage. That's more than half our presidents closely or distantly related.

★ Virginia is the birth state the greatest number of our presidents, including seven of the first twelve — George Washington, Thomas Jefferson, James Madison, James Monroe, William Henry Harrison, John Tyler, and Zachary Taylor, as well as Woodrow Wilson.

★ Ohio is known as the "Mother of Presidents" because eight American presidents were born or lived in Ohio — William Henry Harrison (who lived there when he was elected), Ulysses S. Grant, Rutherford B. Hayes, James Garfield, Benjamin Harrison, William McKinley, William Howard Taft, and Warren Harding.

★ Five candidates for president won the popular vote but lost the election in the Electoral College. In other words, more than 10% of our presidents have not been elected by a majority of our citizens:

Andrew Jackson won the popular vote
           but lost to John Quincy Adams (1824).
Samuel J. Tilden won the popular vote
           but lost to Rutherford B. Hayes (1876).
Grover Cleveland won the popular vote
           but lost to Benjamin Harrison (1888).
Al Gore won the popular vote
           but lost to George W. Bush (2000).
Hillary Clinton won the popular vote
           but lost to Donald Trump (2016).

All five of the above candidates who lost the presidency were Democrats.

★ Between Andrew Jackson and Abraham Lincoln, eight successive presidents served a single term or less:

Martin Van Buren (1837-1841)
           lost re-election to William Henry Harrison.
William Henry Harrison (1841)
           died thirty-one days after his inauguration.
John Tyler (1841-1845) chose not to run for re-election.
James K. Polk (1845-1849)
           chose not to run for re-election.
Zachary Taylor (1849-1850) died in office.
Millard Fillmore (1850-1853) was denied
           nomination for re-election by his party.
Franklin Pierce (1853-1857) was
           denied nomination for re-election by his party.
James Buchanan (1857-1861)
           chose not to run for re-election.

★ One striking pattern of the American presidency is that no woman has occupied that office. It's not that they haven't tried. In 1872, more than a hundred and fifty years ago, Virginia Woodhull, an activist in the suffrage movement, became the first woman to run for president as a member of the National Equal Rights Party. Following the path that Woodhull blazed, other notable women also became candidates for the presidency:

- Belva Lockwood (National Equal Rights Party, 1884 and 1888)
- Shirley Chisholm (Democrat, 1972) - first Black major-party candidate
- Carol Moseley Braun (Democrat, 2004)
- Hillary Clinton (Democrat, 2008 and 2016)
    - first woman nominated by a major party
- Carly Fiorina (Republican, 2016)
- Kamala Harris (Democrat, 2020)
- Tulsi Gabbard (Democrat, 2020 and Independent - 2024)
- Amy Klobuchar (Democrat, 2020)
- Elizabeth Warren (Democrat, 2020)
- Nikki Hailey (Republican, 2024)

In 1984, Geraldine Ferraro (Democrat) became the first woman to run for vice president as the nominee of a major party. Sarah Palin (Republican) did that too in 2008, and in 2020, Kamala Harris became the first woman to be elected vice president.

CHAPTER 21
PRESIDENTS IN THE MEDIA

The cameras never blink.
RONALD REAGAN, *40th president*

Mass media — from portraiture to sculpture, from currency to stamps, from literature to newspapers, from the telephone to radio to television — extend the reputations, images, and sounds of our chief executives and embed them in our national consciousness. And presidents and the governments they lead are usually on the forefront of adopting the latest technology.

★ Campaign slogans and songs existed before William Henry Harrison ran for president in 1840 to unseat Martin Van Buren, but none were employed as successfully as in that campaign.

Harrison was the first presidential candidate to campaign actively — before that, gentlemen did not seek the job; the job sought them — and his catchy campaign slogan "Tippecanoe and Tyler Too" encapsulated a number of ideas in a few words.

In this case, a group of Whig party members rolled a ten-foot-diameter tin and paper ball emblazoned with pro-Harrison slogans more than a hundred miles from Cleveland, Ohio, to Columbus. That stunt gave us the enduring expression "keep the ball rolling" and inspired Alexander Coffman Ross to write his campaign song "Tip and Ty "Tip" was short for Harrison's nickname, "Tippecanoe." Almost thirty years earlier, in 1811,

Harrison, the appointed governor of the new Indiana Territory, led a force of soldiers against the Shawnee Indians, led by Tecumseh and his brother Tenskwatawa. Tecumseh was away recruiting allies to resist American settlement in the territory, but Tenskwatawa and his warriors attacked Harrison's forces on November 7. Harrison and his soldiers won a decisive victory. He became a well-known war hero. The other half of that title, "Ty," was for John Tyler, Harrison's running mate.

What's the cause of this commotion, motion, motion,
Our country through?
It is the ball a-rolling on

For Tippecanoe and Tyler too.
For Tippecanoe and Tyler too.
And with them we'll beat little Van, Van, Van,
Van is a used up man.
And with them we'll beat little Van.

"Little Van" refers to the sitting president, Martin Van Buren, who, at five feet six inches tall, was our second shortest president.

The campaign tactics worked: Harrison won in a landslide. Unfortunately, three weeks after he was inaugurated, in 1841, Harrison fell ill and, nine days later, died. John Tyler became president, and earned a nickname too — "His Accidency."

★ The process of creating daguerreotypes, invented by French artist Louis Daguerre, was cutting-edge technology in 1839. Daguerreotyping was the first photographic process available to the American public. In 1841, Records show that William Henry Harrison was the first president to be photographed. The daguerreotype was made on the day of his inauguration, but like Harrison himself, the image has been lost. John Quincy Adams was photographed in 1843, fourteen years after he left office. James K. Polk was the first sitting president for whom we have an image. He was photographed in 1849 by Matthew Brady, who went on to gain fame for his pictures of the Civil War.

★ Rutherford B. Hayes was an early adopter of telephone technology. He ordered one installed in the telegraph room of the Executive Mansion on May 10, 1877, just over three months after it was patented in January. It connected only to the Treasury Department. Phones were rare in those days. Two years later, there were only 190 entries in the Washington phone book. It was another fifty-two years, during Herbert Hoover's term (1929-1933), before a phone was installed in the oval office.

★ The oldest surviving movie footage of a president is from March 4, 1897. President Grover Cleveland and President-elect William McKinley rode horseback in the procession to the Capitol where McKinley was sworn into office.

★ During the administration of Teddy Roosevelt (1901-1909) a press room was established in the White House during a remodel. Roosevelt didn't hold press conferences, but he made himself available to reporters every day at one o'clock when his barber came to shave him.

★ The first press conference, as we think of it, was on March 15, 1913. Woodrow Wilson (1913-1921) established the tradition and averaged almost seventy-three press conferences a year while in office.

★ The first radio station in America, KDKA in Pittsburgh, went on the air on November 2, 1920. The world's first commercial broadcast occurred to air live returns from the election between Warren Harding and James Cox. They were on the air for eighteen hours and were heard by maybe a thousand listeners.

Nineteen months later, the winner, Warren Harding (1921-1923), was the first president to speak on the radio. On May 30, 1922, he participated in the dedication of the Lincoln Memorial. It's estimated that by 1923, less than one percent of the American public had radio sets, so it's likely Harding had a limited audience, but still bigger than any previous presidential audience.

★ Herbert Hoover (1929-1933) appeared on the nation's first television broadcast in 1927, but as Secretary of Commerce, not as President. He hired the first White House Press Secretary, George E. Akerson, in 1929. Akerson worked for Hoover for two years.

★ The first president to appear on television during his presidency was Franklin Roosevelt. American viewers saw him at the opening of the New York World's Fair on April 30, 1939. He, too, had a limited audience. It's estimated that there were only two hundred televisions in New York City at that time.

★ Roosevelt was also the only president to come close to Woodrow Wilson's record for press conferences. He conducted them twice a week, every week — 992 of them — through wartime and personal illness.

He was famous for his "fireside chats," a series of thirty evening radio talks — one to four per year — given between 1933 and 1944. Originally designed to garner support for his New Deal policies during the Great Depression, Roosevelt broadcast these evening radio talks to the American public straight from the White House. He wanted direct communication with the public without any distortion by the editorial bias of the newspapers. The addresses were designed to give people a sense of hope and security during difficult times and helped keep Roosevelt popular despite the ongoing Depression.

★ On January 19, 1955, Dwight Eisenhower held the first televised press conference.

★ John F. Kennedy was the first president to conduct press conferences on live television, and his successor, Lyndon Johnson, was the first to allow reporters to freely ask questions.

★ The Kennedy-Nixon debates in 1960, watched by seventy million viewers, marked the grand entrance of television into presidential politics. Most experts credit John F. Kennedy's successful TV-friendly performances in the four debates as a significant factor in his subsequent election. Tellingly, most polls indicated that Richard Nixon won the radio versions of those exchanges.

★ The assassination and funeral of John F. Kennedy marked a turning point in American history. It was the first time that virtually the entire nation came together to witness a national tragedy, and the witnessing was through television. The live coverage and images of those events — the shooting of Lee Harvey Oswald, the funeral cortege, the black-veiled widow, and the president's tiny son, John-John, saluting the flag — seared the national psyche and established television as an archetypal source of news.

CHAPTER 22
PRESIDENTIAL STINKERS

Fool me once, shame on you.
Fool me twice, shame on me.
Italian proverb

O ne definition of the word *stinker* is "something extremely difficult." Here follow seven brain-draining presidential stinkers, the answers to which may surprise you.

How many men have been president of the United States?

Although Joe Biden is our forty-sixth president, only forty-five people have held that office. That's because Grover Cleveland was nonsequentially elected as our twenty-second and twenty-fourth president (before and after Benjamin Harrison), irremediably messing up the math.

Who was the youngest man ever to have served as president of the United States?

If your answer is John Fitzgerald Kennedy, you're slightly off the mark. When he took office, Kennedy was, at the age of 43 years and 7 months, the youngest man ever to be *elected* president; but Theodore Roosevelt became president at 42 years and 10 months, in the wake of the assassination of President William McKinley. When TR's second term was over, he was still only fifty years old, making him the youngest ex-president.

Bill Clinton was our third youngest president (46 years and 5 months), followed, by Ulysses S. Grant (46 years and 11 months) and Barack Obama (47 years and 1 month).

Who was the only president born in Illinois?

No, it's not Abraham Lincoln, who was born in Hodgenville, Kentucky. Our only president who started life in Illinois was Ronald Reagan, born in Tampico, Illinois.

Have any of our presidents not been born citizens of the United States?

Yes, eight of them. Martin Van Buren, our eighth president, entered the earthly stage on December 5, 1782, making him the first president born after the Declaration of Independence was signed and thus a citizen. Eight presidents were born before 1776 as British subjects — George Washington, John Adams, Thomas Jefferson, James Madison, James Monroe, John Quincy Adams, Andrew Jackson, and William Henry Harrison.

How many presidents are not buried in the United States?

All those who are still alive.

Can you identify two rock groups, both of which consist of four men, one of whom has the first name of George and another who was assassinated?

The first rock group is the Beatles. The second rock group is — ta-da! — Mount Rushmore. Please take my answer for granite.

Identify a best-selling language writer whose daughter was fired on national television by an American president.

It's Richard Lederer. Back in 2009, his daughter, Annie Duke, then the winningest woman in the history of professional poker, was a contestant on NBC's reality show "Celebrity Apprentice." On the last day of the season, when the apprentices had been winnowed from sixteen to two, then-emcee Donald Trump fired Annie in favor of the comedienne Joan Rivers.

PART V
Manifest Destiny

... the fulfillment of our manifest destiny
to overspread the continent allotted by Providence
for the free development of our yearly multiplying millions.
JOHN L. O'SULLIVAN, *writer, 1845*

CHAPTER 23

LOOK HOW WE'VE GROWN!

America is woven of many strands;
I would recognize them and let it so remain.
Our destiny is to become one, and yet many.
RALPH ELLISON, *writer*

When John L. O'Sullivan coined the term "manifest destiny," he could not have known that his ideas both echoed American thought and would take hold of the American imagination. But they did.

In 1619, the estimated European population of the land that was to become the United States of America was 350 souls.

Article 1, section 2 of the Constitution mandates that an "actual Enumeration" of the nation's population be made every ten years so that "representatives and direct Taxes shall be apportioned among the several States which may be included within this Union, according to their respective Numbers."

By the time the first official census of the thirteen United States occurred, in 1790, we had grown to 3,929,214 residents. Of those, 697,681 were recorded as "slaves," around 17.8% of the population.

No one counted the Native Americans, but historians estimate that between 60,000 and 100,000 lived in the thirteen states, possibly a drop of as much as 90% from the numbers before contact with Europeans. They were not counted until the 1860 census, and not accurately counted until 1890.

Part of the reason they were not counted was logistical — getting to where many Native Americans lived could be difficult, but the other part is that Native Americans and particularly

their claims to land they had lived on for centuries if not mil-
lennia was a barrier to American settlers moving into new territory. Few people wanted to include them in the body politic.
They existed in America as "the other, not us."

Now, the United States of America, a federal constitutional
republic covering 3.79 million square miles, is home to a population of about 330 million people.

Our nation is composed of fifty states; one federal district:
Washington, D.C.; three territories: American Samoa, Guam,
and the U.S. Virgin Islands; and two commonwealths: Puerto
Rico and the Northern Mariana Islands.

Here's a decade-by-decade look at the growth of the American people since 1790:

1800 -	5,308,483	*1910 -*	92,228,496
1810 -	7,239,881	*1920 -*	106,021,537
1820 -	9,638,453	*1930 -*	123,202,624
1830 -	12,866,020	*1940 -*	132,164,569
1840 -	17,069,453	*1950 -*	151,325,798
1850 -	23,191,876	*1960 -*	179,323,175
1860 -	31,443,321	*1970 -*	203,211,926
1870 -	38,558,371	*1980 -*	226,545,805
1880 -	50,189,209	*1990 -*	248,709,873
1890 -	62,979,766	*2000 -*	281,421,906
1900 -	76,212,168	*2010 -*	308,745,538

2020 - 331,449,281

We are one of the world's most urban populations with 83.1% of
us living in cities or suburbs, as compared with a worldwide average
of 56.8%. Since 2010, the number of Americans living in cities has
gone up 3.6%. Less than 2% of the American population live on farms
and ranches and yet raise enough food for the other 98% of us Americans.

As of 2022, our ten most populous American cities were (1) New York (2) Los Angeles (3) Chicago (4) Houston (5) Phoenix (6) Philadelphia (7) San Antonio (8) San Diego (9) Dallas (10) Austin.

★ The population of New York City is upwards of 8.8 million as of 2022, exceeding that of dozens of countries. That figure accounts for about 43 percent of New York State's population.

New York City is not only densely populated (28,000 people per square mile). It is ethnically rich. Its home to the largest number of Dominicans outside the Dominican Republic, the largest number of Jamaicans outside Jamaica, the largest number of Ghanaians outside Ghana, and likely the largest number of Indian Americans and Chinese Americans outside India and China. It's also home to the most Italians outside Italy, Irish outside Ireland, Jews outside Israel, and Puerto Ricans outside Puerto Rico. As a result, New York City is the most linguistically diverse city in the world, with between 700 and 800 languages spoken by residents.

★ The smallest and most densely populated county in America is New York County, which is Manhattan Island. It's only 22.96 square miles, but it contains more than a million and a half denizens. Compare that to the North Slope Borough in Alaska, home of the Iñupiat Eskimos. Almost 95,000 square miles, it's the largest county in the United States. Barrow, its largest city, has a population of 4,500.

★ Los Angeles, our second largest city, has more than 3,800,000 residents. They speak over 224 languages, including, as expected, Spanish and English. Other common languages spoken there are Chinese, Korean, Tagalog, Armenian, Farsi, Russian, French, Italian, and German.

Currently, the U.S. measures slightly more than three million, eight hundred thousand square miles. How did we get to be so big? Well, after the formation of the United States, we started taking and purchasing territory:

★ The Northwest Territory (1787) was west of Pennsylvania, northwest of the Ohio River, and east of the Mississippi River below the Great Lakes. This area covered present-day Ohio, Indiana, Illinois, Michigan, Wisconsin, and part of Minnesota. It was ceded to the United States by England in the Treaty of Paris in 1783. It had previously been part of Quebec.

★ In 1877, during the Revolutionary War, some disputed territory chose to become the independent Vermont Republic· It was admitted to the Union in 1791 as our fourteenth state.

★ With the Louisiana Purchase (1803), we acquired around 828,000 square miles of land from Napoleon's France for $15 million. This acquistion doubled the size of the country. This land included present-day states Louisiana, Arkansas, Iowa, Kansas, Missouri, Nebraska, Oklahoma, North Dakota, and South Dakota, and parts of Colorado, Minnesota, Montana, New Mexico, Texas, and Wyoming. The Louisiana Purchase was negotiated by James Monroe and Robert Livingston, who were then Thomas Jefferson's diplomats in France. Although Monroe later became president, he always considered the Louisiana Purchase to be his greatest achievement.

★ In the Florida Purchase Treaty (1819), Spain gave Florida to the United States in trade for adjustments to the boundary lines between the U.S. and Spanish Texas. Spain was involved in fighting against Spanish American wars of independence and was willing to offload Florida in order to settle the border dispute. Later that year, Mexico gained its independence from Spain and signed a new treaty acknowledging the agreed-upon border. Secretary of State and future president John Quincy Adams negotiated the treaty.

★ The Republic of Texas Annexation took place in 1845. Texas had declared its independence from Mexico in 1836 and then applied for annexation by the United States. The question was complicated by the fact that although slavery was illegal in Mexico, it was legal in Texas, and this was in the time when the problem of the balance of free and slave states in the U.S. was prominent in political discussion. But the discussion was settled, at least temporarily, and Texas came into the union as the twenty-eighth state and as a slave state.

★ Both the United States and Britain claimed ownership of the fur-rich Oregon Country and competed for control, until they finally came to an agreement. The part above the forty-ninth parallel, which would become British Columbia, a province of Canada, went to Britain. The U.S. got the rest, which over time, became the Oregon Territory and then Oregon, Washington, and Idaho, as well as parts of Montana and Wyoming.

★ The Mexican Cession was ceded to the United States after we defeated Mexico in the Mexican-American War (1846-1848). The United States acquired vast territories from Mexico, that became present-day California, Nevada, Utah, most of Arizona, and parts of Colorado, New Mexico, Wyoming.

★ In 1853, the U.S. bought the Gadsden Purchase, a 29,640 square-mile section of present-day Arizona and New Mexico, from the Mexican government in 1853. It was the land south of the Gila River and west of the Rio Grande, which included Yuma, Tucson, and Tombstone. The U.S. wanted to build a Southern railway line through the area, and the Mexicans were broke after the devastating loss of the Mexican

Cession. They may have chosen to sell land they thought might be seized anyway.

★ We weren't finished shopping. We bought the Alaska Purchase from Russia in 1867. Although some called it "Seward's Folly" or "Seward's Icebox" after Secretary of State William H. Seward, most thought it was a good bargain at thirty-six cents an acre for 586,412 square miles. Russia wanted to sell it because they knew they couldn't defend it adequately if Great Britain decided to take it.

★ The Hawaii Annexation occurred 1898. Hawaii is the only state never owned by a foreign nation — unless you count the Americans living in Hawaii as members of a foreign nation. The Hawaiian Islands were an independent kingdom ruled by Queen Lili'uokalani, until a coup d'etat organized by Americans unseated her. The insurgents wanted to be annexed by the U.S., as they ultimately were, in 1898.

In 1993, the U.S. Congress conceded in an apology resolution, long after Hawaii had become a state in 1959, "that the overthrow of the Kingdom of Hawaii occurred with the active participation of agents and citizens of the United States and . . . the Native Hawaiian people never directly relinquished to the United States their claims to their inherent sovereignty as a people over their national lands, either through the Kingdom of Hawaii or through a plebiscite or referendum."

And what about the rest of our country?

★ Guam and Puerto Rico were taken as spoils of war when Spain lost the Spanish American War in 1898. Guam is the largest and southernmost of the Mariana Islands and the largest island in Micronesia in the Southern Pacific Ocean. Puerto Rico is in the Caribbean Sea, near the U.S. Virgin Islands and 1,000 miles southeast of Miami, Florida. Guam is considered an unincorporated territory and Puerto Rico is a commonwealth.

★ The U.S. gained control over American Samoa through the Treaty of Berlin in 1899, which allowed the U.S. to establish a coaling station on the islands. This grew into control of the eastern Samoan islands. It's now an unincorporated territory.

★ The Danish West Indies became the U.S. Virgin Islands when the U.S. bought St. Thomas, St. John, and St. Croix in 1917 from Denmark for $25 million. They became the U.S. Virgin Islands Territory. Just east of Puerto Rico, they are part of the Greater Antilles Archipelago in the Caribbean Sea.

★ The Northern Mariana Islands were part of the Trust Territory of the Pacific Islands removed space administered by the U.S. under a United Nations mandate after World War II. In 1976, they entered into a covenant to become a Commonwealth of the U.S.

CHAPTER 24
THE TRAIL OF TEARS

They made us many promises, more than I can remember,
but they never kept but one.
They promised to take our land, and they took it.
RED CLOUD, *leader of the Oglala Lakota*

There's an old saw that winners write history, and that certainly seems to be true about the relationship between White settlers and Native Americans. There have been two major themes in stories about Native Americans: the noble red man fated to disappear and the villainous Indian who deserved to disappear. Both narratives justified White settlers taking over Native lands, even although the Native Americans, inconveniently, had not yet managed their assigned role.

The American expansion took a terrible cost in lives and suffering. Native Americans paid most of that cost.

A detailed discussion of the sequence of events over the last four hundred years is beyond the scope of this book, but a description of the particular series of events called the "Trail of Tears" can provide some perspective.

Within a lifetime after Europeans first landed in America, they embarked on systematically displacing Native Americans from areas that had potential for farming and mining. The government, first British and then American, seized land and resources. In turn, they promised protection and rights. They provided neither. Officials signed treaty after treaty after treaty and then ignored them. Warfare ensued when Native Americans tried to defend their home territories.

In 1830, The Indian Removal Act passed Congress, and President Andrew Jackson signed it, one of his long time goals.

It gave the federal government the power to trade Indian land east of the Mississippi River for land west of the river (no matter that there were already people long established on that "new" land).

What followed, between 1831 and 1847, was the forcible removal of members of the "Five Civilized Tribes," including approximately 15,000 Choctaw from Mississippi; 3,000 Seminoles from Florida; 15,000 Creek from Georgia and Alabama; 4,000 to 6,000 Chickasaw from Mississippi, Tennessee, and Alabama; and 16,000 Cherokee from Georgia, North Carolina, and Tennessee. They were marched under guard of the U.S. military to the new "Indian Territory" in Oklahoma.

The trip of 500-800 miles took four to six months. Historians estimate that more than 15,000 Native Americans died from starvation, exposure to harsh winter weather, and disease. These numbers are estimates only, as no one kept accurate records. Also, these numbers don't count the Native Americans who died resisting the removal.

The removals opened 25 million acres of land to White settlement.

Along with these relocations, the federal government fought wars against Native Americans. Some, but not all, of the conflicts are listed below.

- (1785-1795) — Northwest Indian War: America against a confederacy of the Miami, Shawnee, Delaware, Ottawa, Potawatomi, Chippewa, Fox, Wea, Kickapoo, Sauk, and Wyandot. (The Old Northwest was the region north of the Ohio River.)
- 1811 — Tecumseh's War: America against a confederacy of the Shawnee, Miami Kickapoo, Delaware, Wyandot, Potawatomi, Sauk, and Fox in the Old Northwest.
- 1817-1858 — Seminole Wars: America against the Seminole in Florida.
- 1820s-1870s — Texas Indian Wars: America against the Comanche, Apache, Kiowa, Wichita, Caddo, Tonkawa, Kickapoo, Seminole, Cherokee, Choctaw, and Chickasaw.
- 1832 — Black Hawk War: America against the Sauk and Fox in the Old Northwest.
- 1862 — Dakota War: America against the Dakota in Minnesota.
- 1863-1865 — Colorado War (including the Sand Creek Massacre). (1863-1865): America against the Cheyenne and Arapaho.
- 1874-1875 — Red River War: America against the Comanche, Kiowa, and Southern Cheyenne in Texas.
- 1876-1877 — Great Sioux War: America against the Sioux in Montana (including the Battle of Little Bighorn), Wyoming, North Dakota, South Dakota, and Nebraska.
- 1877 — Nez Perce War (1877): America against the Nez Perce in Oregon.
- 1851-1924 — Apache Wars: America against the Apache tribes in Arizona, New Mexico, and Mexico.

Apache War Chief Geronimo finally surrendered in 1886, and the government forcibly relocated surviving Native peoples to reservations, ending their traditional ways of life. Small skirmishes continued, and the American military continued to patrol but finally withdrew formally in 1924.

The Indian Wars were over, but the effort to "civilize" Native Americans was not. Authorities created the Indian Boarding School System to strip away the native culture from Native American, Alaska Native, and Native Hawaiian children, to "civilize" the "savages," or as Captain Richard H. Pratt, founder of the U.S. Training and Industrial School in 1879, said, "Kill the Indian; save the man."

Over the years from 1819 to 1969, the government funded 408 schools in thirty-seven states designed to integrate Indian children into American society. Missionaries ran the schools. Attendance was compulsory. Children taken from their families sometimes didn't see them again for as long as four years. Some were as young as four years old. The system systematically stripped of their indigenous identity. They were given new names; their hair was cut; they were required to wear uniforms, not their traditional clothes; church attendance was mandatory; and they were forbidden to speak anything but English, even among themselves. They could not participate in any of their tribal cultural practices. Their education included manual training and indoctrination in Christianity. Discipline was brutal. Physical, emotional, and sexual abuse was rampant. Death rates were high.

Ultimately, as many as 300,000 indigenous children spent time in boarding schools. It wasn't until 1978 that Congress passed a law allowing parents to refuse boarding school for their children.

The Department of the Interior includes the Bureau of Indian Affairs, which in turn manages Indian reservations. In 2021, Secretary of the Interior Deb Haaland announced the

Federal Indian Boarding School Initiative. She said, "I know that this process will be long and difficult. I know that this process will be painful. It won't undo the heartbreak and loss we feel. But only by acknowledging the past can we work toward a future that we're all proud to embrace."

The initiative will create the first official list of federal Indian boarding school sites and will try to identify all marked and unmarked graves at those sites. Then the Interior Department will attempt to mitigate some of the intergenerational trauma caused by its former policies. Perhaps the fact that Haaland is the first Native American to hold a cabinet position in the U.S. government contributed to the department's decision in this matter. Haaland is a member of the New Mexico Pueblo of Laguna.

CHAPTER 25
TRANSPORTATION LINKS THE NATION

Canals, roads, rivers, institutions —
all are of transcendent importance
in binding a nation together
and making every part available to every other.
JOHN LOUDEN McADAM, *civil engineer*

You may know the three R's — "Reading, 'Riting, and 'Rithmatic." But there are another three R's — Rivers, Roads, and Railroads, and they helped America to forge a national identity and culture.

Rivers have been the lifeblood of America since its earliest days, serving as natural highways for exploration, trade, and settlement. Boats, from Native American canoes to modern barges, have been the vessels that allowed Americans to harness the power of our waterways. Long before the advent of railroads, rivers and boats have played a crucial role in shaping American history, from early exploration and settlement to economic development and cultural intermingling Philosopher Blaise Pascal noted, "Rivers are roads that move, taking us whither we wish to go."

The first European explorers and settlers relied heavily on rivers to penetrate the interior of North America. The Hudson, Delaware, and James Rivers on the East Coast became gateways to the continent. French explorers like Marquette and Joliet used the Mississippi River system to explore deep into the heart of America. These waterways allowed for the establishment of early colonies and trading posts, setting the stage for westward expansion. As the nation grew, rivers became crucial arteries of commerce.

The Mississippi River and its tributaries particularly the Ohio River, formed a vast network that connected the agricultural heartland to markets in New Orleans and beyond. Flatboats and keelboats carried crops and goods downstream, while steamboats revolutionized upstream travel in the early nineteenth century. The Erie Canal, completed in 1825, connected the Great Lakes to the Hudson River and New York City, dramatically reducing transportation costs and spurring economic growth in the Northeast. This success led to a canal-building boom, further integrating the nation's waterways.

Rivers and boats weren't just carriers of goods. They also facilitated the movement of people and ideas. The Mississippi River became a fusion of cultures, with French, Spanish, African, and Native American influences blending to create unique riverside communities. Steamboats became floating entertainment venues, bringing music, theater, and news to isolated river towns.

During the Civil War, control of key rivers like the Mississippi became a strategic priority. Ironclad warships and river gunboats played crucial roles in battles and campaigns. The Union's successful control of these waterways was a significant factor in their eventual victory.

The types of boats used on American rivers evolved with technology. Native American dugout canoes gave way to European-style sailing ships. Flatboats and keelboats were succeeded by steamboats, which reigned over river travel and trade for much of the nineteenth century. In the twentieth century, diesel-powered towboats pushing enormous barges became the workhorses of river commerce. While railroads and highways have taken over much of the transportation role once dominated by rivers, water transport remains crucial for moving bulk goods.

The Mississippi River system still carries a significant portion of America's grain exports, and inland waterways continue to be an efficient and environmentally friendly mode of transportation. Rivers and boats have been more than just physical features and tools in American history. They have shaped settlement patterns, driven economic development, and mingled cultural exchange. From the earliest days of exploration to the present, America's rivers and the boats that ply them have been integral to our nation's growth and character.

We often consider the American dream to be to have our own home, to settle, to belong, but we Americans have a second dream nearly as strong — the desire to get out and see the world. The open road beckons and we answer the call. Perhaps Walt Whitman said it best:

Song of the Open Road
Afoot and light-hearted I take to the open road,
Healthy, free, the world before me,
The long brown path before me leading wherever I choose.

Although, perhaps, instead of going to something, we're going away from something else, as Mark Twain's Huckleberry Finn expresses: "But I reckon I got to light out for the Territory ahead of the rest, because Aunt Sally she's going to adopt me and sivilize me, and I can't stand it."

In either case, where there isn't a road, we often make one, as did our ancestors. The first American roads were footpaths between Native American villages and then between colonial villages. For longer distances, rivers served as our pathways.

Although records are spotty and differ in detail, the first paved road in the American colonies may have been parts of the Boston Post Road, a series of Native American trails used to carry mail from Boston to New York. Some records say that parts were paved with cobblestones as early as the 1670s. And while you'd think there would be plenty of rocks in

Massachusetts, those cobblestones probably came into the colonies as ballast in ships. Cobblestones prevented the roads from getting rutted and muddy in rainy weather and dusty in dry weather. They also gave better traction for shod horses.

Dwight D. Eisenhower, former Supreme Commander of the Allied Forces in World War II, was elected president in 1952. The American road system had grown in response to local need, but he saw the importance of an efficient road system, both in promoting commerce and in allowing troop movement in times of emergency.

In his memoir, *Mandate for Change: 1953-1956*, he wrote, "The obsolete road network we inherited from the past, coupled with the geometrically increased demands of the present, meant personnel starvation, bottlenecks, and mind-bending congestion on the very roads that were to have facilitated transportation." Thus began the construction of the interstate highway system, originally called the Dwight D. Eisenhower National System of Interstate and Defense Highways, which we depend on today.

Throughout the nineteenth and early twentieth centuries, the growth of railroads in the United States was another transformative force in our nation's development, driving economic expansion, technological innovation, and social change.

The first commercial railroad in the United States, the Baltimore and Ohio Railroad, began operations in 1830. In the following decades, railroad construction expanded rapidly, particularly in the Northeast and Midwest. By 1850, over 9,000 miles of track had been laid, connecting major cities and facilitating trade. On May 10, 1869, at Promontory Summit, in Utah Territory, a ceremonial 17.6 karat golden spike was driven into the ground to join the rails of the first transcontinental railroad. Now the Central Pacific Railroad from Sacramento and the Union Pacific Railroad from Omaha were now connected, united the United States. The period following the Civil War saw rapid growth in the railroad industry. The 1860s through the 1890s were Golden Age of Railroad Expansion.

The completion of the First Transcontinental Railroad in 1869, linking the East and West coasts, marked a significant milestone. Government land grants and subsidies fueled further expansion, and by 1900, the U.S. boasted nearly 200,000 miles of track. Railroads encouraged economic growth by transporting raw materials and finished goods, which spurred industrial development. Cities grew up around railroad hubs, expanding urbanization and reshaping settlement patterns. Railroad growth peaked in the early twentieth century, but the rise of automobiles and air travel caused a gradual decline in rail transport. Still, the legacy of the railroad era continues to this day to shape American infrastructure and economic geography.

CHAPTER 26
POST OFFICE, TELEGRAPH, AND TELEPHONE

Neither snow nor rain nor heat nor gloom of night
stays these couriers from the swift completion
of their appointed rounds.
U.S. Post Office motto

It's hard to imagine leaving all behind, including the opportunity to communicate with loved ones, but that's what American colonists had to do.

Ship captains and other travelers sometimes carried mail back and forth, and wealthy people hired paid messengers, but there was no official postal service in the American colonies until 1692, when the British Crown appointed an official colonial postmaster.

In 1775, as the Revolutionary War started, the Second Continental Congress appointed Benjamin Franklin as Postmaster General and tasked him with setting up the United States Post Office Service for the rebelling colonies. He held that job until the next year, when he went to France as our ambassador.

Mail followed the frontier. As America grew, so did the Post Office. Delivery reached Louisiana and Missouri by 1804, Florida by 1821, and even California by 1850.

The first adhesive postage stamps were issued in 1847 with Benjamin Franklin on the five cent and George Washington on the ten-cent stamp. They were among the first postage stamps in the world. Previously, the postmaster wrote the postage amount on the corner of the envelope. About 3,700,000 Franklins were printed and about 890,000 Washingtons. A few of the stamps still exist. An unused Franklin stamp is now worth $30,000 to $40,000. The much rarer unused Washington stamp is worth about a half million.

The Post Office hired contractors to carry the mail long distances. They had a contract with the Butterfield Stage Company to carry mail by stage coach from Missouri to California. Stages took about approximately twenty-five days from the end of the railroad in St. Joseph, Missouri 1,900 miles to Sacramento. To speed the process, Butterfield set up the pony express. They carried mail in ten to twelve days. They were faster, but more expensive.

The company set up relay stations about ten miles apart. Young riders would travel about seventy-five to one hundred miles a day changing horses every ten miles. The company went out of business after nineteen months, when the cross-country telegraph lines were completed in 1861.

When the Post Office was originally set up, customers would have to pick up their mail themselves. In 1863, free delivery in major cities was instituted. Mail carriers would carry as much as fifty pounds of mail and walk as many as twenty-two miles a day on their route.

Most Americans, however, lived in villages and on farms. They wanted free delivery too, so the post office set up Rural Free Delivery (RFD) in 1896. Postmen often supplied their own horses and wagons, and sleighs in the winter, to accomplish delivery.

Parcel post began in 1913, when the Post Office raised their limit from four to fifty pounds. If you go to your local post office, you'll see a list of things you may not mail, but people do mail odd things: live animals — for example bees, bugs, and chicks — and dirty laundry back home to Mom.

Between 1913 and 1915, before it was prohibited, people even mailed children from one relative to another. It was cheaper to pay postage than buy a railway ticket.

The first air mail, between Washington, D.C. and New York City, started in 1918. Estimates are that the USPS has handled about 30.5 trillion pieces of mail in its history. In its peak year, 2006, it delivered over 213 billion pieces of mail, or about 703 million pieces a day. Currently, because of competition with email, the average has dropped to about 425 million pieces a day.

The telegraph was another important means of communication. Artist Samuel F. B. Morse (1791-1872) with the help of scientist Leonard Gale invented the telegraph system used in the United States in 1832. It was faster and easier than the systems being developed in Europe. He also created Morse code for transmission of words. In 1837, he received federal money to build a test line between Washington and Baltimore. He spent seven years perfecting his invention, and in 1844, tapped out "What hath God wrought!" a sentence from biblical Numbers 23:23.

Where news and information had taken weeks and then days to share, it now took seconds. This revolutionized the newspaper business, the financial markets, politics, and many other aspects of American life.

Alexander Graham Bell (1847-1922), a teacher of the deaf, came to the U.S. from Scotland in 1871. He patented the first telephone in 1876. The first telephone exchange started in New Haven, Connecticut, in 1878 with twenty-one customers. By 1880, there were fifty thousand telephones in the U.S. and, by 1900, one million.

A transcontinental telephone line was completed in 1914; and on January 25, 1915, Bell placed the first transcontinental telephone call. He was in New York City when he called his close friend and assistant, Thomas A. Watson, in San Francisco. Watson was the same man who had answered Bell's very first telephone call in 1876. Bell had said, "Mister Watson, come here. I want you."

These days, landline phone ownership has steeply declined, with only around 35% of American households owning a landline phone. Around 97% of Americans own some kind of cellphone, and around 85% a smartphone.

Telephone access is now considered essential for most Americans for communication, internet access, navigation, and many other functions built into modern mobile devices.

PART VI
TIES THAT BIND

Despite the differences between us,
there is a unifying American culture
that transcends race, religion, ethnicity, and region.
LANCE MORROW, *author*

CHAPTER 27
AMERICA SINGING

Patriotic songs have the power to unify and inspire,
reminding us of the ideals
that stirred the hearts of our founders.
RENÉE FLEMING, *soprano*

The United States declared war on Britain on June 18, 1812. Most of us know that conflict as the War of 1812, although it lasted from 1812 to 1815. Some historians call it the Second War for American Independence.

Things were going badly for the American side. In 1814, the British captured Washington, D.C., and burned the White House, the Capitol, the Library of Congress, Treasury, State, and War Department buildings, as well as other civic buildings. They marched northeast to Maryland, taking hostages as they went. These hostages, including one Dr. William Beanes, were held on British ships offshore of Baltimore.

Francis Scott Key (1779-1843), a thirty-five-year-old attorney, negotiated for his friend Dr. Beanes's freedom. On the orders of President James Madison, he had the use of a ship and help from American Prisoner Exchange Agent Colonel John Stewart Skinner. Key's negotiations were successful, but his timing was unfortunate. He was aboard a British ship when battle plans were discussed. The captain informed Key that he, Skinner, and Dr. Beanes could not go ashore until the battle was over. They were kept under guard on their own ship for the duration.

Everyone knew that taking Baltimore, an important international port of about 50,000 residents, would effectively split the U.S. in half. British troops on the ground tried but were repelled. After that, it was the British Navy's turn. Their strategy was to take Fort McHenry at the entrance to Baltimore Harbor. If they did that, Baltimore would be undefended from invasion by sea.

Nineteen British ships rode at anchor in Chesapeake Bay just outside the range of Fort McHenry's guns. They started firing before dawn on September 13. Over the next twenty-five hours, they aimed between 1,500 and 1,800 shells and rockets into the fort, killing four Americans and injuring twenty-four.

Baltimoreans had expected the battle and had been readying themselves for months. Major George Armistead, the commanding officer, wanted new flags, including one "so large that the British [would] have no difficulty seeing it from a distance." He got his wish. Mary Pickersgill, a well-known flag maker in Baltimore, made two flags of wool: a smaller storm flag and a larger garrison flag with a hoist (the vertical dimension) of thirty feet and a fly (the horizontal dimension) of forty-two. The stripes of the greater flag were two feet wide, and the stars were two feet from point to point. Since Vermont had joined the union in 1791 and Kentucky had separated from Virginia to become a state in 1792, both flags displayed fifteen stars and fifteen stripes.

Key watched the bombardment from his ship in the Patapsco River. After the battle, he waited anxiously on deck for the sun to rise. He'd seen the storm flag flying the previous night as the sun went down. To his joy, he saw that Armistead had raised the huge garrison flag. The battle for control of Baltimore was over, and the Americans had won. As the sun rose on the scene, Key, an amateur poet, expressed his emotions in a poem that he wrote on the back of a letter. Titled "Defence of Fort M'Henry," those verses were later renamed "The Star-Spangled Banner."

Most Americans know the first stanza:

Oh! say, can you see, by the dawn's early light,
What so proudly we hailed at the twilight's last gleaming?
Whose broad stripes and bright stars,
through the perilous fight,
O'er the ramparts we watched,
were so gallantly streaming?
And the rocket's red glare, the bombs bursting in air,
Gave proof thro' the night that our flag was still there.
Oh! say, does that star-spangled banner yet wave,
O'er the land of the free and the home of the brave?

You can pick up easy money at almost any gathering of American citizenry by wagering that no one can recite any of the ensuing three stanzas. The original copy of Key's poem "Defence of Fort M'Henry" reposes at the Maryland Center for History and Culture: www.mdhistory.org

Star-Spangled Facts

★ The flag that flew over Fort McHenry and inspired Francis Scott Key is on display at the Smithsonian Institution's National Museum of American History in Washington, D. C. After all the rockets' red glare and bombs bursting in air, that flag has eleven holes in it.

★ "The Star-Spangled Banner" was set to the tune of a British drinking song, "To Anacreon in Heaven," and published in Baltimore in 1814 just a few days after Key wrote his poem. It became popular immediately.

★ The Navy first recognized "The Star-Spangled Banner" for official government use in 1889, to be played at reveille, when the flag is raised.

★ It wasn't until 1916 that President Woodrow Wilson declared by executive order that "The Star-Spangled Banner" was the national anthem, to be played at all military installations.

★ On March 3, 1931, by congressional resolution, "The Star-Spangled Banner" became our official national anthem.

★ The motto "In God We Trust" may have been adapted from a line in the fourth stanza of "The Star-Spangled Banner": "And this be our motto — 'In God is our Trust.'" It first appeared on a U.S. two-cent piece in 1864. Over the years, the words were added to more coins, and since 1938, all coins have carried the motto. "In God We Trust" became the official motto of the United States in 1956 and started appearing on paper currency in 1957.

America Set to Music

We Americans love to sing about our country. Most of us know the tune and at least the opening lyrics to the likes of "When Johnny Comes Marching Home Again," "Battle Hymn of the Republic," "My Country 'Tis of Thee," "You're a Grand Old Flag," and the rousing rhythm of John Phillip Sousa's marches such as "Stars and Stripes Forever."

★ The first verse of "Yankee Doodle," as often sung today, runs:

Yankee Doodle went to town,
Riding on a pony.
He stuck a feather in his hat
And called it macaroni.

The original Yankees were Dutch settlers who came to the New World and settled in the area around the future New York City and the Hudson River Valley. *Yankee* may derive from the Dutch *Jan Kaas*, "Johnny Cheese." The word migrated from an ethnic insult against the Dutch to being against New Englanders in general as a pre-Revolutionary creation sung by British military officers. The intent of "Yankee Doodle" was to mock the ragtag, disorganized New Englanders with whom the British served in the French and Indian War (1754-1763).

Doodle first appeared in the early seventeenth century and derives from the Low German word *dudel,* meaning "fool" or "simpleton." The macaroni wig was in high fashion in the 1770s and became contemporary slang for foppishness. The last two lines of the first verse implied that the unsophisticated Yankee bumpkins thought that simply sticking a feather in a cap would make them the height of fashion.

The colonists liked the tune of "Yankee Doodle" and adopted it as a robust marching song. What was once a derisive musical ditty became a source of American pride.

★ Katherine Lee Bates (1859-1929), a professor of English at Wellesley College, wrote the lyrics to the soaring song "America the Beautiful." While she taught in Colorado in the summer of 1893, the view of Pike's Peak inspired her to write her poem. Although Bates never met New Jersey church organist Samuel A. Ward, the music of his hymn "Materna," composed in 1882, was combined with her poem and first published together in 1910.

★ Composer and lyricist Irving Berlin (1888-1989) wrote "God Bless America" in 1918 while serving in the army at Camp Upton in Yaphank, New York. Berlin created the song for a revue of his titled *Yip Yip Yaphank*, but he set it aside because he decided that the piece was too solemn for his otherwise comedic show. Twenty years later, as the shadow of Adolf Hitler rose to darken the world, Berlin, a first-generation Jewish immigrant from Russia, decided to revise his handiwork from a victory song to a peace song.

Contralto Kate Smith (1907-1986), backed by full orchestra and chorus, introduced the song on a 1938 Armistice Day radio broadcast. It became an instant hit and Smith's signature song during her long career. For a while, there was even a movement to make "God Bless America" our national anthem.

CHAPTER 28
HAPPY HOLIDAYS

Our national holidays provide opportunities
to reflect on shared heroes, unite around common hopes,
and celebrate the remarkable creed
that binds us as one American family.
BARACK OBAMA, *44th president*

Although this chapter is titled "Happy Holidays" — and we're all happy to get a day off from time to time — holidays can also be solemn. Holidays celebrate the best of us. To call something a national holiday makes it sound like the whole country takes the day off, but in fact, national holidays are for federal government employees. Congress established the first four national holidays — New Year's Day, Independence Day, Thanksgiving Day, and Christmas Day — in 1870 for employees in nonessential offices in the District of Columbia. They extended it to all federal employees in 1885, and the number of holidays has expanded from four to eleven. Other organizations, such as state and local governments, businesses, and schools, have chosen to follow the federal government's lead.

★ New Year's Day is now celebrated on January 1, but it wasn't always so. Great Britain, Wales, Ireland, and Britain's American colonies adopted January 1 as New Year's Day starting in 1752. Previously, the new year had been celebrated on March 25. The same parliamentary law of 1750 that established the New Year also switched the British Empire from the older Julian calendar to the more accurate Gregorian calendar. In 1582, Pope Gregory XIII had decreed the creation of this calendar to keep the civil year aligned more closely with the tropical year (the time between vernal equinoxes) and to recalibrate the date of Easter for the Roman Catholic Church. It took Britain a hundred and seventy years before they finally followed suit.

The adoption of that calendar required the elimination of eleven days in 1852. People went to bed on September 2 and woke up on September 14. This meant, for example, that under the Julian calendar, George Washington celebrated his birthday on February 11. Under the Gregorian calendar, he and we celebrate it on February 22, and because the new year moved to January 1, the year he was born changed too. He was now born in the beginning of 1832 rather than at the end of 1831.

★ Martin Luther King Jr. Day was established in 1983. His actual birthday was January 15, 1929, but we celebrate it on the third Monday of January. The day honors King, a leader in the African American civil rights movement. He used non-violent resistance and civil disobedience to fight for voting and labor rights and against racial discrimination and poverty. In 1965, he received the Nobel Peace Prize, one of twenty-two Americans and one American organization awarded that honor since 1901. He died by assassination on April 4, 1968.

★ You'll be glad to know that George Washington's Birthday is still George Washington's Birthday, at least in the federal calendar. It was established as a holiday, celebrated on his actual birthday — February 22 — in 1879. In 1971, the federal holiday shifted to the third Monday in February because of the Uniform Monday Holiday Act, designed to give federal workers three-day weekends. Memorial Day, Veterans Day, and Columbus Day also shifted to Mondays. Later, Veterans Day shifted back to November 11, and Martin Luther King Day was added. Labor Day has always been on a Monday, so that makes five long weekends for federal employees.

Although federally it's George's holiday, in some states, that day honors Washington and Abraham Lincoln (born February 12, 1809). Still others celebrate Washington, Lincoln, and Thomas Jefferson (born April 13, 1743). Finally, some places call it Presidents Day, with or without an apostrophe. You can evidently honor anyone you want, but the day officially belongs to Washington, the man justifiably called "The Father of Our Country."

★ Cesar Chavez Day is a U.S. federal commemorative holiday, proclaimed by President Barack Obama in 2014. The holiday celebrates the birth and legacy of the farm worker, labor leader and civil rights activist who co-founded what is now known as the United Farm Workers union. It celebrates Chavez's birthday on March 31 and is observed in six states.

★ Memorial Day, then called Decoration Day, started in 1866 as an unofficial day to honor and mourn the Union dead of the Civil War. Mourners decorated graves with flowers. It was observed on different days in different places. In 1868, we made it a formal holiday, observed on May 30. After the world wars, the observance was widened to honor all the military personnel who died in service.

Since 1971, we call it Memorial Day and observe it on the last Monday in May. We now honor approximately 1.4 million men and women who have died in service to our country. Early records are spotty, but the number of wartime dead we mourn are as follows:

- Revolutionary War: estimated 25,000 Patriot deaths
- Civil War: estimated 620,000 deaths
- World War I: 116,516 deaths
- World War II: 405,399 deaths
- Korean War: 36,516 deaths
- Vietnam War: 58,209 deaths
- Gulf War: 383 deaths
- Post-9/11 Wars (through 2022): Around 7,057 deaths
- Other deaths in service since 1775: 200,000 (estimated).

Two other days honor military service. Armed Forces Day (not a national holiday) honors those currently serving in the Army, Navy, Marine Corps, Air Force, Space Force, Coast Guard, Reserves, and National Guard (approximately 2,450,000 as of 2022). Veterans Day, which is a national holiday (see below), honors all veterans, living and dead.

★ Juneteenth National Independence Day is our newest national holiday, as of 2021. Celebrated on June 19, it reminds us of June 19, 1865, the day that Major General Gordon Granger ordered the freedom of the quarter of a million enslaved people in Texas at the end of the Civil War. The slaves in Galveston Bay are thought to be the last in the U.S. to hear that they had been freed. They had to wait two-and-a-half years after President Lincoln issued the Emancipation Proclamation, an executive order that freed all slaves in the Confederate States, to get the news. Slaves in Union states didn't get their freedom until the Thirteenth Amendment to the Constitution became law in December 1865.

Churches and social groups began celebrating that freedom the next year, 1866. The observance spread across the country as formerly enslaved Blacks and their descendants migrated north and west to take advantage of new opportunities. The holiday is often celebrated by a reading of the Emancipation Proclamation, and groups join to sing a hymn, written in 1900 by Black poet James Weldon Johnson and his brother, J. Rosamond Johnson, that has been called the Black national anthem:

Lift Every Voice and Sing

Lift every voice and sing,
'Til earth and heaven ring,
Ring with the harmonies of liberty;
Let our rejoicing rise
High as the listening skies,
Let it resound loud as the rolling sea.
Sing a song full of the faith that the dark past has taught us,
Sing a song full of the hope that the present has brought us;
Facing the rising sun of our new day begun,
Let us march on 'til victory is won.
Stony the road we trod,
Bitter the chastening rod,
Felt in the days when hope unborn had died;
Yet with a steady beat,
Have not our weary feet
Come to the place for which our fathers died.
We have come, over a way that with tears has been watered,
We have come, treading our path
Through the blood of the slaughtered,

Out from the gloomy past,
'Til now we stand at last
Where the white gleam of our bright star is cast.
God of our weary years,
God of our silent tears,
Thou who has brought us thus far on the way;
Thou who has by Thy might
Led us into the light,
Keep us forever in the path, we pray.
Lest our feet stray from the places,
Our God, where we met Thee,
Lest our hearts drunk with the wine of the world,
We forget Thee;
Shadowed beneath Thy hand,
May we forever stand,
True to our God,
True to our native land.

★ Independence Day, popularly known as the Fourth of July, commemorates the day the Second Continental Congress ratified our Declaration of Independence from Great Britain. It's one of the most festive occasions of the year. On that day, we celebrate the freedom of the thirteen colonies that broke away from England and formed the United States of America. We remember the signing of the Declaration of Independence, which expressed the desires of the new American citizens and proclaimed their belief in three basic rights — life, liberty, and the pursuit of happiness.

So this coming summer, halfway between Memorial Day and Labor Day, as you're getting out your festive red, white, and blue decorations or eating a hot dog at a barbecue or cheering at a baseball game or gawking at spectacular fireworks, stop for a moment and think about the almost quarter of a million Patriots who fought in the eight years of the Revolutionary War. They endured many hardships and spilled their blood so that we could live in the freedom that we enjoy today. Without their bravery and will to stand up to England and fight for their right to be free, our United Sates of America would be a much different place.

★ Labor Day became an official federal holiday in 1894. We celebrate it on the first Monday in September. It honors the contribution of American workers and the labor movement to our economy. Labor unions pushed for the federal holiday and then encouraged workers to strike to have the holiday spread to other jurisdictions and organizations. It worked, and now almost everyone celebrates the day.

The day marks the unofficial end of summer, as Memorial Day marks the beginning. For some, then, it's the last day to wear white shoes until the following Memorial Day. For others it's an important day of remembering and celebrating with family and friends.

★ Holidays are not necessarily without controversy, both personal and political. Columbus Day is a good example. It celebrates Columbus's first landfall in the New World. He went ashore at Guanahani in the Bahamas on October 12, 1492 after three months at sea. As Americans began to realize that the Americas were "discovered" thousands of years before 1492 by people we now call Native Americans, a wide discussion has begun on whether Columbus caused more harm than good. Although it's still Columbus Day for the federal government and has been since 1971, some other jurisdictions have begun calling it Indigenous People's Day, Native American Day, or similar names. Some places don't mark it at all.

★ Veterans Day was established as a federal holiday in 1954. Previously, it had been called Armistice Day and celebrated the end of World War I, "the war to end all wars," on the eleventh hour of the eleventh day of the eleventh month, November 11, 1918. Now, it honors all veterans, living and dead, of the armed services — Army, Navy, Marine Corps, Air Force, Space Force, and Coast Guard. We celebrate it on November 11, unless that falls on a weekend, in which case, we celebrate on the nearest Friday or Monday.

★ George Washington established the first national celebration of Thanksgiving on November 26, 1789. After that, it was celebrated sporadically in different areas of the country. It wasn't until 1863, in the midst of the Civil War, that Abraham Lincoln, hoping to unite a sundered nation, issued a proclamation declaring Thanksgiving a national holiday to be celebrated that year on the last Thursday of November. He did this at the urging of Sarah Josepha Hale, the poet and magazine editor who wrote the children's rhyme "Mary Had a Little Lamb" and who had been lobbying for years to establish the holiday.

After that, each president designated the day when Thanksgiving would be celebrated. It could be different with each administration. Franklin Roosevelt moved turkey day up a week to the third Thursday in November — to give Americans more time for Christmas shopping. Controversy followed, and Congress passed a joint resolution in 1941 decreeing that Thanksgiving should fall on the fourth Thursday of November, where it remains.

★ Christmas is the only religious federal holiday in a country that values separation of church and state. As such, many people do not celebrate it at all or celebrate it only as a secular holiday. No matter. They still get the day off.

Humans have long celebrated the winter solstice (December 21-22), when the sun reaches its farthest south position and starts "moving" north again. Christmas, Yule (neo-pagan and Wiccan), Soyal (Hopi), Shap-e Yalda (Iranian), Dong Zhi (East Asian), Lohri (Hindu), and other celebrations in the U.S, mark the time when human beings yearn for stories of light shining down on them bringing hope during the darkest time of the year. So while Christmas is the most widely observed, there are many other cultural, religious, and folkloric holidays concentrated around the December winter solstice period.

CHAPTER 29
FOOD, GLORIOUS FOOD

The greatest thing about food is its ability
to bring people together.
GUY FIERI, *chef*

O ne of the threads that weaves us together into families,
communities, and a nation is food. We gather in homes,
restaurants, fellowship halls, parks, sports stadiums, and at the
beach for potlucks, picnics, group dinners, and quiet family
meals. Almost every family occasion and form of entertainment
includes food as a component.

But is there such a thing as an American palate? Do you
know what muktuk is or johnnycake? Have you eaten poi?
Hummus? Moose hash? Lo mein? Mountain oysters? Gefilte
fish? Some of us would say yes, most of us, no. But we all do
know what hamburgers, hot dogs, and french fries are.

When colonists first entered what later became the United
States, they found native cuisines that included many foods they
hadn't seen before. They incorporated these foods into their
daily diets and went on to develop new local foodways:

- turkey
- dried beans such as kidney, lima, navy, and pinto beans
- peanuts
- sunflower seeds
- hazelnuts, pecans, and black walnuts
- maple, birch, and hickory syrup
- wild rice

- corn, potatoes, tomatoes, avocados, several types of chili peppers
- blueberries, huckleberries, service berries, cranberries; chokecherries, persimmons, pawpaws, pumpkins, and squash
- sassafras, sumac, allspice, vanilla, wild ginger, bergamot, pot herbs, such as lamb's quarters and purslane, and juniper berries.

In 1796, Amelia Simmons pioneered the development of a new American cuisine. She wrote a cookbook, *American Cookery*, the first cookbook authored by an American and published in the United States. It adapted recipes from Native American, English, French, and Dutch cuisines using ingredients that were native to America. It included recipes for such things as "pompkin" pudding served in a crust, cranberry sauce, and gingerbread. It helped create a distinct American culinary identity.

Each region of the United States still boasts its own cuisine, but some foods we've developed are now found nationwide and even worldwide. It's hard to imagine a town, a village, or a hamlet in America where you couldn't get a hamburger and french fries. And what do you drink? A soft drink. You may call it pop, soda, tonic, or Coke, depending on where you live, but it's everywhere.

★ Somebody once defined a hamburger as "a humble im- migrant hunk of meat that came to this country and soared to fame on a bun." That somebody was right. The hamburger, named after a city in Germany, began life in Europe as *Hamburg steak*, ultimately shortened to hamburger. In 1891 in Tulsa, Oklahoma, the hamburger patty first snuggled into a bun.

And then came the fast food restaurant. White Castle originated the concept in 1921, to be followed by A&W Root Beer in 1923 and Dairy Queen in 1940.

McDonald's also started in 1940. It had humble beginnings. The first McDonald's was a San Bernardino, California, drive-in opened in 1940 by two brothers, Richard and Maurice McDonald. They prepared and sold a large volume of hamburgers, french fries, and milk shakes using assembly-line production.

Ray Kroc (1902-1984) sold milk shake mixers to the brothers. Kroc partnered with them in 1954 to help with franchising, eventually buying them out in 1961 for one million dollars apiece. Commenting that a hamburger restaurant named Kroc's wouldn't attract many customers, Kroc opened his first new McDonald's in 1955 in Des Plaines, Illinois. Then he began selling franchises. Now there are almost 40,000 restaurants worldwide One of his many innovations was the training program he instituted for owner- managers — Hamburger University in Oak Brook, Illinois.

In 2022, by revenue, McDonald's was the largest fast food chain in the world, with system wide sales of around $112 billion. It ranks second among all restaurant/food service companies globally by revenue, behind only Starbucks.

 ★ Another classic Americanism is the hot dog. When hot sausages in a bun became popular, it was but a short leap to the term *hot dog*, the idea being that the sausage looks like a small, short-legged, long-bodied dachshund wiener dog.

★ There is a dispute among food historians as to whether french fries were actually created in France or in Belgium, but there's no dispute about where potatoes came from — South America. They were first planted in the U.S. in New Hampshire in 1719. There are records of a White House dinner in 1802, where Thomas Jefferson presented "potatoes served in the French manner." They didn't seem to catch on, though, until they were brought back to the U.S. by World War I soldiers who had eaten them in Belgium. Later, they were popularized by the fast food restaurants that blossomed all over America from the 1950s on. In 2022, American farmers harvested almost forty billion (yes, with a "b") pounds of potatoes. Twenty-seven percent of those potatoes became french fries.

★ In 1787, our first foodie president, Thomas Jefferson, introduced pasta to the United States. When he served as ambassador to France, he grew to love the taste of pasta so much that he ordered a pasta-making machine sent back to the U.S., the first "macaroni maker" in America. Quite the gourmet, Jefferson is also credited with introducing anchovies, olive oil, and Parmesan cheese.

★ Soda has a long history in America. We consume more than fifty gallons of the sweet, fizzy stuff per person per year. In 1806, Benjamin Silliman sold the first artificial mineral water in New Haven, Connecticut. The first soda fountains were manufactured in the 1830s; and in 1898, Dr. Pepper started bottling its product and distributing it across the country. You're probably familiar with orange, grape, and lemon-lime. Maybe you've tried black cherry or grapefruit. But what about pineapple, green apple, or peach? Not wild enough? How about honeydew, watermelon, huckleberry, marionberry, or kumquat? Still too tame? Then there's celery, cucumber, lavender, ginseng, rhubarb, and juniper berry. There are even sodas that mimic the harder stuff— mojito, Chianti, amaretto, lime rickey, and julep.

Coca-Cola, the world's number-one soft drink, originally contained cocaine, which came from one of its ingredients, coca leaves. All the cocaine was removed after 1905. The caffeine, which came from cola nuts, remained. Coke has 1/6 to 1/3 the amount of caffeine as an equal amount of coffee, depending on the bean and brewing method.

Pepsi-Cola was named Brad's Drink when Caleb Bradham created it in 1893. He was trying to concoct a fountain drink that would aid digestion and boost energy. In 1898, he changed the name to Pepsi-Cola, based on the ingredients, pepsin and Kola nuts.

Bib-Label Lithiated Lemon-Lime Soda, created in 1929, changed its name to 7Up. It's easy to see why that mouthful was condensed.

★ In 1718, the first published recipe for ice cream appeared in England in *Mrs. Mary Eales's Receipts*, but techniques for making ice cream were known long before that.

To Make Ice Cream

Take Tin-Ice-Pots, fill them with any Sort of Cream you like, either plain or sweeten'd, or Fruit in it; shut your Pots very close; to six Pots you must allow eighteen or twenty Pound of Ice, breaking the Ice very small; there will be some great Pieces, which lay at the Bottom and Top: You must have a Pail, and lay some Straw at the Bottom; then lay in your Ice, and put in amongst it a Pound of Bay-Salt; set in your Pots of Cream, and lay Ice and Salt between every Pot, that they may not touch; but the Ice must lie round them on every Side; lay a good deal of Ice on the Top, cover the Pail with Straw, set it in a Cellar where no Sun or Light comes, it will be froze in four Hours, but it may stand longer; then take it out just as you use it; hold it in your Hand and it will slip out.

The confection probably reached the American colonies in the early 1700s. In 1790, George Washington paid $200, a hefty sum in those days, for ice cream equipment and recipes. Two presidents later, in 1802, Thomas Jefferson had a special recipe for vanilla ice cream and became the first to serve ice cream in the White House.

To see Jefferson's handwritten Recipe go to:
https://www.loc.gov/resource/mtj1.056_0146_0146/

★ We Americans are definitely sweet in the tooth. In addition to gulping down vats of soda, and gallons of ice cream, we ingest tons of candy. In 2024, the per capita candy consumption in the U.S. was 22 lbs. Did you receive your share of candy kisses, Valentine conversation hearts, Peeps, jellybeans, chocolate Easter eggs, and candy corn?

★ Fortune cookies are an American invention, and they have a surprisingly dark history. Created for Japanese, not Chinese, restaurants in America, they're patterned on wafer cookies made in Kyoto, Japan, but use different ingredients. The first ones were probably served at a Japanese tea garden in San Francisco in 1908. Gradually they came to be served in both Japanese and Chinese restaurants.

In 1960, manufacture of the cookies was automated, and their popularity took off. Currently, manufacturers bake about three billion fortune cookies a year, and most are eaten in the U.S. You may have noticed that the strips of paper nestled inside fortune cookies are frequently not fortunes. Messages such as "He who throws dirt is losing ground," "Big journeys begin with a single step," and "I hear and I forget. I see and I remember. I do and I understand" do not foretell the future.

★ SPAM, a blend word for spiced ham, is manufactured in Austin, Minnesota, and Fremont, Nebraska. The product was introduced in 1937. Because fresh meat was hard to find in World War II, soldiers often found it in their rations. They brought their fondness for it home with them. The eighth billionth can was sold in 2012, and 244 million cans were sold in the U.S. in 2017. It's now sold in forty-one countries and is so popular on the Pacific islands of Guam, Hawaii, and Saipan that McDonald's restaurants there feature SPAM.

★ Americans spend more than $6.4 billion a year on ready-to-eat cereal. The Cheerios brand accounts for one in every eight boxes sold in the U.S. General Mills debuted CheeriOats in 1941 and changed the name to Cheerios four years later. The little o's are made with puffing gun technology, in which balls of dough are heated and shot out of a gun at hundreds of miles an hour to create the iconic, round shape.

★ The U.S. is one of the largest producers of apples in the world. The Roxbury Russet apple is probably the first named American apple. It has been grown here since the mid-1600s and is good for eating and for making juice and cider. It may have been one of the apples planted by Johnny Appleseed.

Far from being a whimsical ne'er-do-well as portrayed in movies and popular literature, John Chapman (1774-1845), also known as Johnny Appleseed, was a trained nurseryman and a canny businessman who started a series of plant nurseries on the frontier. Johnny planted apple trees and left them in the care of local residents. Once a year or so, he would drop by to tend the trees and divide profits with his representative.

Thus, he had an essential product waiting when settlers arrived. In 1800, he started selling apple seedlings to settlers in Pennsylvania, Ohio, Indiana, Illinois, and Kentucky. Over the course of his lifetime, Chapman was responsible for planting more than a hundred thousand acres of apple orchards across our land.

Apples don't grow true from seed. That means if you have a wonderful apple tree and you plant the seeds, you won't get another wonderful apple tree. You'll probably get apples that are just about inedible. That didn't matter to Johnny or to his customers. They weren't buying eating apples; they were buying apple trees for cider making. Hard cider was the beverage of choice at a time when water was unsafe.

CHAPTER 30
OUR NATIONAL PASTIME

I think there are only three things
America will be known for 2,000 years from now
the Constitution, jazz music, and baseball.
GERALD EARLY, *professor of African American studies*

A merica is a sports loving nation. Throughout their lives, Americans invest considerable money, time, and passion in playing sports and following the exploits of teams and individual athletes. Most schools and colleges are represented by a coterie of sports teams, and the morale of a major city rises and falls with the successes and stumbles of its school and professional teams.

The three most popular spectator team sports in this country — football, basketball, and baseball — started in North America. I can't cover all sports within the brief compass of this book, so I'll focus on baseball, which has justly been called "the national pastime."

"To understand America, you must understand baseball." This statement, attributed to several writers, goes on to say "Baseball is our game: the American game. That game is the picture of Democracy at work. Look at the players — White, Black, Jewish, Irish, German, Italian. Look at the spectators — likewise from all particulars. Baseball gives a glimpse of America en masse." This unknown author saw baseball as representative of American culture, diversity, and democratic values.

★ Games like baseball started in England and then, with a variety of names such as rounders, town ball, wicket, and base ball, came to the North American colonies, including Canada, with their settlers.

★ It's probable that the first surviving recorded use of the term "baseball" in the U.S. dates to a law passed in 1791 in Pittsfield, Massachusetts:

ByeLaw for the Preservation of the Windows in the New Meeting House.

Be it ordained by the said Inhabitants that no Person, an Inhabitant of said Town, shall be permitted to play at any Game called Wicket, Cricket, Baseball, Batball, Football, Cat, Fives, or any other Game or Games with Balls within the Distance of Eighty Yards from said Meeting House.

★ The first official record of a game comes from fifty-five years later, when on June 19, 1846, in Hoboken, New Jersey, the New York Nine defeated the Knickerbockers, 23–1, in four innings. The Knickerbocker written rulebook set the parameters at the time, although the rules have continued to evolve.

★ As the rules have changed, so has the technology. radio, TV, and airplanes have expanded the audience for the game. Artificial turf, such as Astroturf, improved field maintenance. The use of computerized scouting, pitch tracking, and instant replay have changed recruiting and training.

★ The Cincinnati Red Stockings were the first professional team, declaring their professional status in 1869. The National League formed in 1876, and the American League followed in 1901.

★ Professional Baseball spread from the U.S. and is now played in eighteen countries — Australia, Canada, China, Colombia, Cuba, the Dominican Republic, Germany, Italy, Japan, Mexico, the Netherlands, Nicaragua, Panama, Puerto Rico, South Korea, Sweden, Taiwan, and Venezuela. Other countries have semi-pro and amateur leagues. Players from many countries have played for American teams over the years starting as early as 1871.

★ Like much of life, baseball has inspired many works of art. Examples include "Baseball Players" by Thomas Eakins (1888), "Hartland Artist" by Frederic Remington (1892), "The Phillies Clinching the Pennant" by Norman Rockwell (1948), "Baseball" by Alexander Calder (1966), and "The Baseball Catch" by Elaine de Kooning. Sculptors, too, are taken with the grace and drama of the game and provide works such as "The Catcher" by Harriet Hosmer (1859) and "The Strike" by Ernie Barnes (1970). Photographers have created such pictures as "The Mutt at Home Plate" by Charles Conlon (1909) and Ansel Adams's photographs of baseball games in Yosemite National Park in the 1920s.

Baseball is a common theme in literature too, with books such as *The Natural* by Bernard Malamud (1952), *Ball Four* (1970) by Jim Bouton, and *The Boys of Summer* (1972) by Roger Kahn. Even theater and movies have had their time at bat: *The Pride of the Yankees* (1942), *Damn Yankees* (1955), *Bull Durham* (1988), *Field of Dreams* (1989), and *A League of Their Own* (1992).

This list barely touches the surface. Here's one more example. Ernest Lawrence Thayer's well-known poem appeared in 1888 and remains popular today:

Casey at the Bat

The outlook wasn't brilliant for the Mudville nine that day;
the score stood four to two, with but one inning more to play.
And then when Cooney died at first, and Barrows did the same,
a sickly silence fell upon the patrons of the game.

A straggling few got up to go in deep despair. The rest
clung to that hope which springs eternal in the human breast;
they thought, if only Casey could get but a whack at that —
they'd put up even money, now, with Casey at the bat.

But Flynn preceded Casey, as did also Jimmy Blake,
and the former was a lulu and the latter was a cake,
so upon that stricken multitude grim melancholy sat,
for there seemed but little chance of Casey's getting to the bat.

But Flynn let drive a single, to the wonderment of all,
and Blake, the much despised, tore the cover off the ball;
and when the dust had lifted, and the men saw what had occurred,
there was Jimmy safe at second and Flynn a-hugging third.

Then from five thousand throats and more there rose a lusty yell;
it rumbled through the valley, it rattled in the dell;
it knocked upon the mountain and recoiled upon the flat,
for Casey, mighty Casey, was advancing to the bat

There was ease in Casey's manner as he stepped into his place;
there was pride in Casey's bearing and a smile on Casey's face.
And when, responding to the cheers, he lightly doffed his hat,
no stranger in the crowd could doubt 'twas Casey at the bat.

Ten thousand eyes were on him as he rubbed his hands with dirt;
five thousand tongues applauded when he wiped them on his shirt.
Then while the writhing pitcher ground the ball into his hip,
defiance gleamed in Casey's eye, a sneer curled Casey's lip.

And now the leather-covered sphere came hurtling through the air,
and Casey stood a-watching it in haughty grandeur there.
Close by the sturdy batsman the ball unheeded sped —
"That ain't my style," said Casey. "Strike one," the umpire said.

163

From the benches, black with people, there went up a muffled roar,
like the beating of the storm-waves on a stern and distant shore.
"Kill him! Kill the umpire!" shouted someone on the stand;
and it's likely they'd have killed him had not Casey raised his hand.

With a smile of Christian charity great Casey's visage shone;
he stilled the rising tumult; he bade the game go on;
he signaled to the pitcher, and once more the spheroid flew;
but Casey still ignored it, and the umpire said: "Strike two."

"Fraud!" cried the maddened thousands, and Echo answered fraud;
but one scornful look from Casey and the audience was awed.
They saw his face grow stern and cold, they saw his muscles strain,
and they knew that Casey wouldn't let that ball go by again.

The sneer is gone from Casey's lip, his teeth are clenched in hate;
he pounds with cruel violence his bat upon the plate.
And now the pitcher holds the ball, and now he lets it go,
and now the air is shattered by the force of Casey's blow.

Oh, somewhere in this favored land the sun is shining bright;
the band is playing somewhere, and somewhere hearts are light,
and somewhere men are laughing, and somewhere children shout;
but there is no joy in Mudville — mighty Casey has struck out.

★ With more than a century and a half of American history, baseball evokes more nostalgia than any other athletic endeavor. No other sports song is nearly as famous as "Take Me Out to the Ball Game," a Tin Pan Alley creation of Jack Norworth and Albert Von Tilzer, first recorded in 1908. Now fans typically sing it during the seventh-inning stretch.

Take Me Out to the Ball Game

Katie Casey was baseball mad,
Had the fever and had it bad.
Just to root for the home town crew,
Ev'ry sou Katie blew.
On a Saturday her young beau
Called to see if she'd like to go
To see a show, but Miss Kate said, "No,
I'll tell you what you can do:"

Chorus
Take me out to the ball game,
Take me out with the crowd;
Buy me some peanuts and Cracker Jack
I don't care if I ever get back.
So let's root, root, root for the home team
If they don't win, it's a shame.
For it's one, two, three strikes, you're out,
At the old ball game.

Katie Casey saw all the games,
Knew the players by their first names.
Told the umpire he was wrong,
All along, good and strong.
When the score was just two to two.
Katie Casey knew what to do,
Just to cheer up the boys she knew,
She made the gang sing this song:

★ More fans than in any other sport know the key statistics of baseball — most hits (Pete Rose, 4,256); most wins (Cy Young, 511); most strikeouts (Nolan Ryan, 5,714); most home runs in a season and over a career (Barry Bonds, 73,762); most stolen bases (Ricky Henderson, 1,406); most consecutive games played (Cal Ripken, Jr., 2,632); and on and on and on. All these men are in the Baseball Hall of Fame in Cooperstown, New York.

★ In 1947, Jackie Robinson joined the all-White Brooklyn Dodgers and broke Major League Baseball's color barrier. In 1945, he'd led the racially segregated Kansas City Monarchs of the Negro American League to the World Series championship. That season, he had a batting average of .387 with 16 home runs. His performance caught the attention of Branch Rickey, manager of the Dodgers. Rickey wanted to break the color barrier, and Robinson's talent and temperament made him an ideal candidate.

In 2020, the centennial of the first Negro League, Major League Baseball agreed the racially segregated Negro Leagues were as "major" as the National and American Leagues and integrated the statistics of the four leagues. With the statistics of the players in the Negro Leagues now included in the history of baseball, thirty-seven of its stars are now enshrined in the National Baseball Hall of Fame including the cream of the crop Leroy Robert "Satchel" Paige, Walter "Buck" Leonard, James Thomas "Cool Papa" Bell, William Julius "Judy" Johnson, and Oscar Charlton.

Legendary catcher Josh Gibson is now the MLB's leader in career batting average of .372, surpassing Ty Cobb's .367, and career slugging percentage .718, overtaking Babe Ruth's .690.

★   And because baseball occupies such a central place in American life and imagination, it's the source of some of the most pervasive athletic metaphors in our language. Whether or not we're fans, we speak baseballese, as witness the following conversation:

Jack picked up the project folder from his desk and joined Jill to walk down the hall. *"I can't get to first base* with this proposal I'm writing, *I'm stuck out in left field with two strikes* against me."

She smiled. "Cheer up. I'm confident you'll be *a smash hit* and *you'll step up to the plate, swing for the fences,* and *hit a home run."*

"I'm not so sure." He shook his head. "You know our boss. She runs *a major league operation,* and she *plays hardball."*

"Huh!" Jill said. "I think she's a *screwball,* and she runs a *bush-league* business. What's your biggest problem?"

"Well, *right off the bat,* I can't even come up with a solid cost estimate."

"You're always *in there pitching,* Jack. Just give her *a ball-park figure."*

"I will." Jack nodded. "Thanks for *batting around* these ideas with me."

"Touch base with me anytime. I'm always ready to *go to bat* for you."

"That's so sweet, Jill. Can I take you out to a ball game?"

Jill smiled "Thanks, but I'll take a *raincheck."*

Jack squared his shoulders as he walked into the boss's office.

CHAPTER 31
THE SILVER SCREEN

Nothing can tell you more about America than the movies.
SIDNEY LUMET, *film director*

Americans have fallen deeply in love with that beguiling conspiracy of light and darkness and color and silence and sound and music that we call the movies. Movie megastar Matt Damon says it this way: "Movies are one of the few things that bind us, that allow people to experience the same dreams and memories when they're sitting in a theater."

The Great Train Robbery, an eleven-minute, silent, black-and-white film produced in 1903, was the first to tell an extended story. It was also the first commercially successful film, earning $150.00, big bucks back then. This "western" was actually shot in New Jersey, our nation's film capital until the more benign weather of Los Angeles lured away the filmmakers.

In 1927, Warner Brothers Studio released *The Jazz Singer,* the first feature-length film with synchronized speech and sound effects. Its star was Al Jolson (1886-1950). Jolson sang six songs in the movie, but there were only two minutes of spoken dialog. That was enough. The audience was electrified by what it heard. Silent movies were on the way out.

In the movie theater — and increasingly on smaller screens — the boundaries between real and reel, the line between reality and movies, wavers and blurs. Something has happened to our American language — and I've a feeling we're not in Kansas anymore.

METRO-GOLDWYN-MAYER'S TECHNICOLOR TRIUMPH!

WE'RE OFF TO SEE THE WIZARD...
THE WONDERFUL...

WIZARD OF OZ

Judy GARLAND • Frank MORGAN
Ray BOLGER, Bert LAHR, Jack HALEY

You'll probably recognize the second part of that statement as a borrowing from the film *The Wizard of Oz.* Being transported out of Kansas is one of a passel of expressions from movies that have launched a thousand lips.

The very first Academy Awards ceremony took place during a banquet held in the Blossom Room of the Hollywood Roosevelt Hotel. Two hundred and fifty attended and tickets cost $10. When the first awards were handed out on May 16, 1929, movies had just begun to talk. I would love to have been a time traveler rushing into the Blossom Room to announce the luminous future of the Academy Awards ceremony:

"Wait a minute! Wait a minute! You ain't heard nothing yet!" That's what Al Jolson said in *The Jazz Singer* (1927), the mother of all talking films. Ever since, lines from the movies have shaped our hopes and dreams and aspirations and have suffused our everyday conversations.

Today I'm making you an offer you can't refuse — a version of the line in Mario Puzo's novel, *The Godfather*, published in 1961, and embedded in the 1972 film of the same name.

So what's up, Doc? That is, of course, from Bugs Bunny's characteristic question to Elmer Fudd. What's up is that I hope never to hear from you readers, "What we have here is a failure to communicate" or "I'm mad as hell, and I'm not going to take this anymore!"

The first statement began as a line in *Cool Hand Luke*, and the second is Peter Finch's furious complaint in *Network*.

May you never sneer at me, "Frankly, my dear. I don't give a damn," spoken by Clark Gable in *Gone with the Wind*. But that's okay because tomorrow is another day.

Indeed, I think this is going to be the beginning of a beautiful friendship, a line delivered by Humphrey Bogart in *Casablanca*. That film also gave us "Round up the usual suspects" and "Here's looking at you, kid."

Plunge ahead, gentle reader, and you'll go ahead, make my day — the signature statement of the Clint Eastwood character Dirty Harry in the 1983 film, *Sudden Impact*, a line made even more famous by President Ronald Reagan.

You'll make my day because love is never having to say you're sorry, an enduring sentiment from *Love Story*.

So, who you gonna call? — your faithful American history author! That's a spin-off from *Ghostbusters,* and, of course, it should be "whom are you going to call?"

Now identify the films whence came the following expressions that inhabit our everyday conversations:

1. They're ba-a-a-ck!
2. If you build it, they will come.
3. Houston, we have a problem.
4. Life is like a box of chocolates.
5. You talkin' to me?

6. I coulda been a contender!
7. Why don't you come up sometime and see me?
8. This could be the end of civilization as we know it.
9. May the Force be with you!
10. Show me the money!

11. I'll have what she's having.
12. Here's Johnny!
13. You're gonna need a bigger boat.
14. I'm king of the world!
15. There's no crying in baseball!

Answers

1. *Poltergeist* 2. *Field of Dreams* 3. *Apollo 13* 4. *Forrest Gump* 5. *Taxi Driver*
6. *On the Waterfront* 7. *She Done Him Wrong* 8. *Citizen Kane* 9. *Star Wars* 10. *Jerry Maguire*
11. *When Harry Met Sally* 12. *The Shining* 13. *Jaws* 14. *Titanic* 15. *A League of Their Own*

That's all, folks! *Hasta la vista,* baby! — and you know where those two lines got their start: "Merry Melodies" and *Terminator 2: Judgment Day*

PART VII
OUR AMERICAN LANGUAGE

The American language is
the legitimate production of a nation,
and should be cherished
as such by every citizen.
NOAH WEBSTER, *lexicographer*

CHAPTER 32

A DECLARATION

OF LINGUISTIC INDEPENDENCE

England and America are two countries
separated by a common language.
GEORGE BERNARD SHAW, *playwright*

Beginning with the Pilgrims, the story of language in America is the story of our Declaration of Linguistic Independence, the separating from its parent of that magnificent upstart we call American English.

John Adams was one of the first to lead the charge for American linguistic autonomy. In 1780, sixteen years before he became president, he called upon Congress to establish an academy for "correcting, improving, and ascertaining the English language." "English," Adams proclaimed, "is destined to be in the next and succeeding centuries more generally the language of the world than Latin was in the last or French is in the present age. The reason of this is obvious, because the increasing population in America, and their universal connection and correspondence with all nations, will, aided by the influence of England in the world, whether great or small, force their language into general use."

At the time Adams made that prediction, an obscure Connecticut schoolmaster was soon to become a one-man academy of American English. His name, now synonymous with the word *dictionary,* was Webster. Noah Webster (1758-1843) saw the untapped promise of the new republic. He was afire with the conviction that a United States no longer politically dependent on England should also become independent in language. In his

Dissertations on the English Language, published in 1789, Webster declared linguistic war on the King's English: "As an independent nation, our honor requires us to have a system of our own, in language as well as government."

In putting his vision into practice, Noah Webster traveled throughout America, listening to people's speech and taking detailed notes. He included in his dictionaries an array of shiny new American words, among them *applesauce, bullfrog, chowder, handy, hickory, succotash, tomahawk* — and *skunk:* "a quadruped remarkable for its smell." Webster also proudly used quotations by Americans to illustrate and clarify many of his definitions. The likes of Ben Franklin, George Washington, John Jay, and Washington Irving took their places as authorities alongside William Shakespeare, John Milton, and the Bible. In shaping the American language, Webster also taught a new nation a new way to spell. He deleted the *u* from words such as *honour* and *labour* and the *k* from words such as *musick* and *publick,* he reversed the last two letters in words such as *centre* and *theatre,* and he Americanized the spelling of words such as *plough (plow)* and *gaol (jail).*

Perhaps no one has celebrated this "American dialect" with more passion and vigor than the poet Walt Whitman. "The Americans are going to be the most fluent and melodious-voiced people in the world–and the most perfect users of words," he predicted before the Civil War. "The new world, the new times, the new people, the new vistas need a new tongue. What is more, they will . . . not be satisfied until it is evolved."

From the Age of Queen Anne (1702-1714), the British have thundered against what one of their magazines called "the torrent of barbarous phraseology" that poured from the American colonies. The first British broadside launched against an Americanism is recorded in 1735, when an English visitor named Francis Moore referred to the young city of Savannah as standing upon a hill overlooking a river "which they in barbarous English call a bluff."

The British were still beating their breasts over what the *Monthly Mirror* called "the corruptions and barbarisms which are hourly obtaining in the speech of our trans-Atlantic colonies," long after we stopped being colonies. They objected to almost every term that they did not consider standard English, protesting President Jefferson's use of the verb *belittle.* They expressed shock at the American tendency to employ, in place of *suppose,* the likes of *expect, reckon, calculate,* and — a special target — *guess,* conveniently overlooking Geoffrey Chaucer's centuries-old "Of twenty yeer of age he was, I gesse."

Returning from a tour through the United States in the late nineteenth century, the playwright Oscar Wilde jested, "We really have everything in common with America nowadays except, of course, language."

But our home-grown treasure Mark Twain put it all into perspective when he opined about American English, as compared with British English: "The property has gone into the hands of a joint stock company, and we own the bulk of the shares."

CHAPTER 33
NATIVE TONGUES

English has undressed
and then drest up in buckskin
from Delaware and Narragansett wardrobes.
JOHN LAWSON, *explorer, 1709*

MOre than four centuries ago, the roots of Thanksgiving first took hold in our American soil. We living today commemorate the solemn dinner, back in the fall of 1621, shared by the Pilgrims of Plymouth, Massachusetts, and the Wampanoag Indians, the local tribe who generously pulled the fragile Pilgrim colony through their first winter and taught them how to plant corn. (In the early seventeenth century, corn was seen in England as an exotic novelty crop. The pilgrims would not have known that it could be used for food. Native Americans, though, had been growing it for centuries.)

Suppose you were one of the early settlers of North America. You would have found many things in your new land unknown to you. The handiest way of filling voids in your vocabulary would have been to ask the locals what words they used. The early colonists began borrowing words from Native Americans almost from the moment of their first contact, and many of those names have remained in our everyday language:

In a letter that British explorer John Smith wrote home in 1608, he described a critter that the Virginia Algonquians called a *rahaughcum* or an *aroughcan,* "he scratches with his hands." Over the years the word was shortened and simplified to *raccoon,* one of the very first English words coined in America.

Pronouncing many of the Native American words was difficult for the early explorers and settlers. In many instances, they had to shorten and simplify the names. Identify the following animals from their Native American names:

apossoum (Don't play dead now.)
ockqutchaun (How much wood?)
seka-kwa (What's black and white and stinks all over?)

The hidden animals are *opossum, woodchuck,* and *skunk.* To this menagerie, you can add the likes of *caribou, cayuse, chipmunk, coyote, husky, iguana, moose, muskrat,* and *quahog (clam).*

You can also diversify your menu with Native words for food — *avocado, chocolate, guacamole, hickory, hominy, jalapeño, jerky, pecan, pemmican, persimmon, potato, squash,* and *succotash.*

And think about the number of our words that describe Native American culture and technology — *hogan, igloo, kayak, moccasin, mugwump, powwow, tepee, toboggan, tomahawk, totem, wampum,* and *wigwam.*

If you examine a map of the United States, you will realize how freely settlers used words of Indian origin to name the places where we live. Rivers, lakes, ponds, creeks, mountains, valleys, counties, towns, and cities as large as Chicago (from a Miami-Illinois word *Shikaakwa* that means "place of wild onions") bear Native American names.

Four of our five Great Lakes — Huron, Ontario, Michigan, and Erie — and twenty-five of our states have names borrowed from Native American words: *Alabama, Alaska, Arizona, Arkansas, Connecticut, Idaho, Illinois, Iowa, Kansas, Kentucky, Massachusetts, Michigan, Minnesota, Mississippi, Missouri, Nebraska, North Dakota* and *South Dakota, Ohio, Oklahoma, Tennessee, Texas, Utah, Wisconsin, and Wyoming.*

Some of our loveliest place names began as Native American names — *Susquehanna, Shenandoah*, and *Rappahannock*. Such names are the stuff of poetry.

"The poet Henry Wadsworth Longfellow wrote, "The Indians have given us beautiful names, poetic names, having the quality almost of music, for all the places where they lived."

Author Constance Fenimore Woolson observed, "How rich and mellifluous are the Indian names, like fountains of liquid silver spelling down the mountains." How fortunate we are that the poetry the indigenous people heard in the American landscape lives on in our American language.

CHAPTER 34
THE PRESIDENTIAL ORIGIN OF *Okay*

"It's okay to make mistakes.
Mistakes are our teachers."
JOHN BRADSHAW, *counselor*

W hat may be the most useful expression of universal communication ever devised, *OK* is recognizable and pronounceable in almost every language on earth.

The explanations for the origin of *OK* have been as imaginative as they have been various. But the late language maven Allen Walker Read proved that *OK* did not derive from *okeh,* an affirmative reply in Choctaw; nor from the name of chief Old Keokuk; nor from a fellow named Orrin Kendall, who manufactured a tasty brand of army biscuit for Union soldiers in the Civil War and stamped them *OK*; nor from the Haitian port Aux Cayes, which produced superior rum; nor from "open key," a telegraph term; nor from the Greek *olla kalla,* "all good."

Rather, as Professor Read pointed out, the truth is more political than any of these theories. He tracked down the first known published appearance of *OK* with its current meaning in the Boston *Morning Post* on March 23, 1839: "The 'Chairman of the Committee on Charity Lecture Balls' is one of the deputation, and perhaps if he should return to Boston, via Providence, he of the Journal, and his train-band, would have the 'contribution box,' et ceteras, o.k.–all correct–and cause the corks to fly, like sparks, upward."

Allen Walker Read demonstrated that *OK* started life as an obscure joke and through a twist of fate went to the top of the charts on the American hit parade of words. In the 1830s, in New England, there was a craze for initialisms, in the manner of *LOL, OMG, aka,* and *TGIF,* so popular today. The fad went so far as to generate letter combinations of intentionally comic misspellings: *KG* for "know go," *KY* for "know yuse," *NSMJ* for "'nough said 'mong jentlemen," and *OR* for "oll rong." *OK* for "oll korrect" naturally followed. Of all those loopy initialisms and jocular misspellings *OK* alone survived. That's because of a presidential nickname that consolidated the letters in the national memory. Martin Van Buren, elected our eighth president in 1836, was born in Kinderhook, New York, and, early in his political career, was dubbed "Old Kinderhook." Echoing the "Oll Korrect" initialism, *OK* became the rallying cry of the Old Kinderhook Club, a Democratic organization supporting Van Buren during the 1840 campaign. Thus, the accident of Van Buren's birthplace rescued *OK* from the dustbin of history.

The coinage did Van Buren no good, and he was defeated in his bid for re-election. But *OK* has become what H. L. Mencken identified as "the most shining and successful Americanism ever invented."

PART VIII
HOMEGROWN AUTHORS

Reading makes a full Man,
Meditation a profound Man,
Discourse a clear Man.

BENJAMIN FRANKLIN, in *Poor Richard's Almanack*

CHAPTER 35
EARLY BEST-SELLERS

Books are the quietest and most constant of friends.
They are the most accessible and wisest of counselors.
CHARLES WILLIAM ELIOT, *president of Harvard, 1869-1909*

Like our American language, American literature created itself from the raw materials of frontier life in the New World, not from the literary traditions of the Old World. Our national literature is an evolving multicultural tapestry of Romanticism and Transcendentalism, Realism and Naturalism, and Modernism and Postmodernism. Join us for a brief tour of a gallery of American authors who shaped our literature.

Estimates tell us that between 10 and 20 percent of early settlers in what would become the United States were literate. Most of those who were literate were wealthier White men. Literacy rates were much lower for women, enslaved people, and Native Americans. Those who were literate read to others, and their main source was the Bible. Published sermons and religious texts were also popular.

A reading textbook, the *New England Primer*, first published between 1687 and 1690, sold over two million copies in the eighteenth century. Many were sold in Massachusetts and Connecticut, where parents were required by law to teach their children to read so that they could read the Bible. Literacy rates rose over the decades.

Here are the kinds of books that were popular during that time period:

Courtesy books, which taught etiquette, such as *Youths Behavior, Or, Decency in Conversation Amongst Men* (1646) by

Francis Hawkins. This book was popular through the seventeenth and eighteenth centuries.

Conduct books, which taught proper moral conduct, such as *Essays to Do Good* (1710) by Cotton Mather.

Histories such as *The History of the Province of Massachusetts-Bay* from 1749-1774 (1828) by Thomas Hutchinson.

Almanacs, like *Poor Richard's Almanack* published every year from 1732 to 1758 by Benjamin Franklin. Franklin's other books were popular too: *Experiments and Observations on Electricity* (1751), *The Way to Wealth* (1758), and the *Autobiography of Benjamin Franklin* (first published in French in 1791).

Other important publications in the 1700s include "Common Sense," (1776) and the *Federalist Papers* (1787-1788). "Common Sense," a pamphlet by Thomas Paine, sold more than a half million copies. It called for American Independence. *The Federalist Papers,* originally published as *The Federalist: A Collection of Essays, Written in Favour of the New Constitution, as Agreed upon by the Federal Convention, September 17, 1787,* included eighty-five essays written by Alexander Hamilton, James Madison, and John Jay under the pen name "Publius." The essays were designed to promote the ratification of the Constitution.

The nineteenth century brought a rising rate of literacy and new challenges and interests. American authors had an outsized influence on the beliefs and hopes of our populace. Writers from different regions and life experiences strengthened a unifying national literature and American identity: Their ideas live on long after they have passed.

CHAPTER 36
AN AMERICAN VOICE EMERGES

The creation of an authentic American voice in literature
was one of the essential labors of the democratic experiment.
MALCOLM BRADBURY, *critic*

As the nineteenth century spooled out, fresh voices shaped
an American literary tradition and forged an American
identity. Authors grappled with profound questions as they
searched for truth and meaning in life in our country.

★ Henry David Thoreau (1817-1862) helped runaway
slaves escape to Canada and became one of the first Americans to speak in defense of radical abolitionist and outlaw
John Brown. When Thoreau spent a day in jail for acting on
the dictates of his conscience, he was visited by friend Ralph
Waldo Emerson. Emerson asked, "Henry, why are you here?"
Thoreau answered, "Waldo, why are you not here?"

In Walden, Henry David Thoreau followed the tenets of
American Transcendentalism by living in the woods and shar-
ing his vigorous advocacy of civil liberties in his essay Civil
Disobedience. He advanced American ideals like individual-
ism, simplicity, and principled resistance.

Thoreau's passion for social issues like slavery, economy, politics, and nature speaks to us across the centuries. Both Ma-
hatma Ghandi, who fought for Indian independence from England, and Martin Luther King Jr., who fought for Black civil
rights in America, modeled their activism on Thoreau's "Civil

Disobedience." Thoreau's observations of nature and man's place in and impact on nature inspired environmentalists like John Muir.

★ *Leaves of Grass*, a collection of poems by Walt Whitman (1819-1892), is a landmark of American literature. He first published it in 1855 and spent the next thirty-three years revising it, adding new poems, and republishing it. He signaled a radical departure from established norms, including a voice that spoke in the first person directly to readers, and captured the energy and diversity of our burgeoning nation. He was revered by other poets in his lifetime and to the present day. Critics of the day were less kind. They found much of his poetry to be obscene. When the first edition appeared, the Boston Intelligencer said in its review: "The poet should be kicked out from all decent society as below the level of the brute. He must be some escaped lunatic raving in pitiable delirium." The collection went through nine more editions and gained a large, enthusiastic readership in the United States and England.

Whitman's poem "Oh Captain, My Captain," mourning the death of Abraham Lincoln, was his only poem anthologized during his lifetime. Among his most famous poems are "I Hear America Singing" and "I Sing the Body Electric" which celebrated our country's spirit. Walt Whitman indeed bequeathed America a voice to sing of itself.

I Hear America Singing

I hear America singing, the varied carols I hear,
Those of mechanics, each one singing his
as it should be blithe and strong,
The carpenter singing his
as he measures his plank or beam,
The mason singing his
as he makes ready for work, or leaves off work,
The boatman singing what belongs to him in his boat,
the deckhand singing on the steamboat deck,
The shoemaker singing as he sits on his bench,
the hatter singing as he stands,
The wood-cutter's song,
the ploughboy's on his way in the morning,
or at noon intermission or at sundown,
The delicious singing of the mother,
or of the young wife at work,
or of the girl sewing or washing,
Each singing what belongs to him or her and to none else,
The day what belongs to the day —
at night the party of young fellows, robust, friendly,
Singing with open mouths their strong melodious songs.

★ On the night of April 20, 1910, Halley's Comet shone in the skies as it made its closest approach to the earth. Just a year before, Samuel Clemens, who wrote under the name Mark Twain (1835-1910) said to a friend: "I came in with Halley's Comet in 1835, and I expect to go out with it. The almighty has said, no doubt, 'Now here go these two unaccountable frauds; they came in together, they must go out together.' Oh! I am looking forward to that." One day later, April 21, 1910, Samuel Clemens escaped the bounds of earth.

But Mark Twain, the most American of American writers, did not go out with Halley's Comet. In *The Adventures of Huckleberry Finn, The Adventures of Tom Sawyer*, and so many other books, he wrote in an American grain, creating quintessentially American characters, American landscapes, and American dialects. He closed the breach that yawned between literary grandiosity and the American vernacular his characters actually spoke.

Ernest Hemingway said of Twain, "All modern American literature comes from one book by Mark Twain called *Huckleberry Finn*. It's the best book we've had."

CHAPTER 37
THE DIVERSITY
OF OUR MODERN LITERATURE

The new literature of shared American experience
admits not one absolute voice
but the chorus of many voices, many cultures.
GISH JEN, *novelist*

Writers from various times, regions, and life experiences, have strengthened a unifying national literature and American identity:

★ In her novels, including *My Ántonia*, and *O Pioneers!*, Willa Cather (1873-1947) illuminated the immigrant experience when she portrayed the frontier lives of settlers on the American plains, telling timeless tales of strong pioneer women facing extraordinary challenges.

★ Robert Frost (1874-1963) is generally recognized as the premier American poet of the twentieth century. His base was always life in Northern New England, and no one else has ever captured more vividly the essence of that corner of our country, but his only boundaries are the trackless regions of the human condition.

Stopping by Woods on a Snowy Evening

Whose woods these are I think I know.
His house is in the village though;
He will not see me stopping here
To watch his woods fill up with snow.

My little horse must think it queer
To stop without a farmhouse near
Between the woods and frozen lake
The darkest evening of the year.

He gives his harness bells a shake
To ask if there is some mistake.
The only other sound's the sweep
Of easy wind and downy flake.

The woods are lovely, dark and deep,
But I have promises to keep,
And miles to go before I sleep,
And miles to go before I sleep.

★ *The Grapes of Wrath*, by Nobel-Prize-winner John Steinbeck (1902-1968), became the most widely read depiction of life in the Great Depression. Steinbeck's other books, including *Of Mice and Men* and *Cannery Row*, focused on the lives of America's downtrodden.

★ Langston Hughes (1902-1967) was the first Black writer in America to create a strictly literary career. In 1924, when he was a young busboy in a Washington, D. C., hotel, he left a packet of his poems next to the poet Vachel Lindsay's plate.

Lindsay helped to launch the young man's career, and the bus-boy became the leading figure in the Harlem Renaissance. Hughes was an artist and innovator who bestowed on his poetry a new tone, infused with Black life and Black language.

I, Too

I am the darker brother.
They send me to eat in the kitchen
When company comes,
But I laugh,
And eat well,
And grow strong.

Tomorrow,
I'll be at the table
When company comes.
Nobody'll dare
Say to me,
"Eat in the kitchen,"
Then.
Besides,
They'll see how beautiful I am
And be ashamed —

I, too, am America.

197

★ Rachel Carson (1907-1964), was an aquatic biologist and passionate nature writer. Her *Silent Spring* and other books alerted an unprecedented audience to the environmental, animal, and human damage wrought by the indiscriminate use of DDT and other pesticides. Her work inspired a grass-roots movement that led to the creation of the Environmental Protection Agency.

★ In his novels, essays, plays, and poetry, James Baldwin (1924-1987) spoke brutally and eloquently about the complexity of race in America. He understood that he couldn't single-handedly change the world but believed that literature could illuminate truths, provoke thought, and inspire change. With moral power, he also elucidated homosexuality, bisexuality, and interracial relationships, taboo subjects in his day.

★ In her novel *To Kill a Mockingbird*, Harper Lee (1926-2016) painted an enduring portrait of racial injustice in the American South in the 1930s. Narrated by a young girl, Scout Finch, the story unfolds as her father, Atticus Finch, a principled lawyer, defends Tom Robinson, a Black man falsely accused of raping a White woman.

★ Novelist, poet, essayist, and painter N. Scott Momaday (1934-2024) was the first Native American to win a Pulitzer Prize. Combining his reverence for the complex culture of his Kiowa heritage with a classical university education, he inspired a renaissance of Native American literature.

★ African American culture and vernacular and feminist themes suffuse the novels, short stories, and poems of Alice Walker (1944-). Cele, the main character in her most famous novel, *The Color Purple*, survives rape and abuse at the hands of her father and husband and separation from her children and sister to find love with another woman.

PART IX
THE LAUGHS ARE ON US

Humor is the great thing, the saving thing after all.
The minute it crops up, all our hardnesses yield,
all our irritations, and resentments flit away,
and a sunny spirit takes their place.
MARK TWAIN, *writer*

Literary humor; radio, TV, and newspaper comedy; and political and social satire are bright threads in the fabric of American culture. Our humor reflects the diverse ethnic and cultural perspectives of our people. At the same time comedy serves as a unifying force through shared laughter. As musical comedian Victor Borge put it, "Laughter is the shortest distance between two people."

We begin to learn the humor of our social group at an early age. How many people remember when they first heard "What's black and white and read/red all over?" The answer: a newspaper. That archetype led to additional answers: a zebra with diaper rash, an embarrassed penguin, a nun who spilled catchup on herself, and on and on.

The wordplay in a good joke or riddle surprises and delights us, and we always want to share it with others. To close this book, I offer the lighter side of American history through American riddles:

★ What is the most fruitful subject to study in school?
History. It's full of dates.

★ How do we know that Columbus was the best deal maker in history?
He left not knowing where he was going. When he got there, he didn't know where he was. When he returned, he didn't know where he'd been. And he did it all on borrowed money.

★ How do we know that Columbus's ships got the best gas mileage in history?

They got three thousand miles per galleon.

★ If April showers bring May flowers, what do Mayflowers bring?

Pilgrims.

★ Why did the Pilgrims' pants always fall down?

Because they wore their buckles on their hats.

★ What was the Pilgrims' favorite kind of music?

Rock.

★ Which colonists told the most jokes?

Punsylvanians.

★ What was the favorite dog in colonial times?

The Yankee Poodle.

★ What protest by a group of dogs occurred in 1773?

Boston Flea Party.

★ What do you call a bunch of cattle gathered in a space satellite?

The herd shot 'round the world.

★ What did Benjamin Franklin's political opponents say when they got angry at him?

"Go fly a kite!"

★ Why did Paul Revere ride his horse from Boston to Lexington?

Because the horse was too heavy to carry.

★ Where was the Declaration of Independence signed?

At the bottom.

★ Why did the duck say, "Bang!" on the Fourth of July?

Because he was a firequacker.

★ What did King George think of the American colonists?

He found them revolting.

★ What did the colonists call the barnyard fowl they trained to capture British spies?

Chicken catch-a-Tory.

★ What has four legs, a shiny nose, and fought for England?

Rudolph the Redcoat Reindeer.

★ What would you get if you crossed George Washington with cattle feed?

The Fodder of Our Country.

★ What would you get if you crossed our first president with a wood sculptor?

George Washington Carver.

★ What decision did George Washington make about how to cross the Delaware?

Roe v. Wade.

★ Plagued with bad teeth, what did our first president wear in his mouth?

The George Washington Bridge.

★ If George Washington were alive today, why couldn't he throw a silver dollar across the Potomac River?

Because a dollar doesn't go as far as it used to.

★ What is the difference between a duck and George Washington?

The duck has a bill on his face and Washington has his face on a bill.

★ What's big, cracked, and carries your luggage?

The Liberty Bell-hop.

★ Did you hear the joke about the Liberty Bell?

Yeah, it cracked me up.

★ What did one flag say to the other flag?

Nothing. It just waved.

★ What's red, white, blue, and yellow?

The Star-Spangled Banana.

★ What do you call the tigers, skunks, and zebras that hang out with Tarzan?

The Tarzan stripes.

★ Did you hear about the cartoonist in the Continental Army?

He was a Yankee doodler.

★ What dance was very popular in 1776?

The Indepen-dance.

★ What happened as a result of the Stamp Act?

The Americans licked the British.

★ What's red, white, black, and blue?

Uncle Sam falling down the steps.

★ What's red, white, blue, and green?

A patriotic pickle.

★ How is a healthy person like the United States?

They both have good constitutions.

★ What was Thomas Jefferson's favorite musical instrument?

The Monti cello.

★ What would you get if you crossed the American national bird with Snoopy?

A bald beagle.

★ Which American president is the least guilty?

Abraham Lincoln. He's in a cent.

★ What was Jefferson Davis voted in his high school year-book?

Most likely to secede.

★ What do an owl and our sixteenth president have in common?

They're both A'blinkin'.

★ What do George Washington, Abraham Lincoln, and Martin Luther King Jr. have in common?

Each was born on a holiday.

★ How can we tell that the Statue of Liberty loves America?

She carries a torch for us.

★ What kind of electricity do they have in Washington?

D.C.

★ What message did Alexander Graham Bell receive when he made the first telephone call?

"Your call is important to us. Please continue to hold. Your call will be answered in the order it was received and may be monitored for quality control."

I powerfully hope that future generations will know enough about American history to laugh at riddles and jokes like the ones you've just read.

About the Author

Richard Lederer is the author of more than sixty books about language, history, and humor, including his best-selling Anguished English series and his current titles, *Lederer's Language and Laughter* and *A Feast of Words* He is a founding co-host of "A Way With Words," broadcast on Public Radio.

Dr. Lederer's column, "Lederer on Language," appears in newspapers and magazines throughout the United States. He has been named International Punster of the Year and Toastmasters International's Golden Gavel winner.

He lives in San Diego with his wife, Simone van Egeren.

richardhlederer@gmail.com/verbivore.com

Acknowledgments

I thank Josh Freel for designing the front and back covers of *American History for Everyone;* Charles and Eileen Patton for formatting the text and interior illustrations; and Howard Killion, Deb Stone, Debbie Lee, Karl Albrecht, and Eileen Patton for serving as beta readers.

Made in the USA
Las Vegas, NV
03 November 2024

11087892R00125